RIDING THE FENCE REALLY HURTS!

Embrace GOD'S Plan for Your Life

www.judy-bowen.com

Judy Bowen

Creative Team Publishing
Fort Worth, Texas

© **2021 by Judy Bowen.**

All rights reserved. No part of this book may be reproduced, stored in a retrieval system or transmitted in any form or by any means without the prior written permission of the publisher, except by a reviewer who may quote brief passages in a review distributed through electronic media, or printed in a newspaper, magazine, or journal.

Disclaimers:
- o Due diligence has been exercised to obtain written permission for use of references, quotes, or imagery where required. Any additional quotes, references, or imagery may be subject to the Fair Use Doctrine. Where additional references, quotes, or imagery may require source credit, upon written certification that such a claim is accurate, credit for use will be noted on this website: **www.judy-bowen.com**
- o The opinions and conclusions expressed herein are solely those of the author and/or the individuals and entities represented. This book is a book of religious faith in God. It includes Judy's personal story and journey of faith, as well as her reliance upon Him as Sovereign Lord.
- o Views and opinions are quoted with permission. Opinions and conclusions are limited to the telling of the facts, experiences, and circumstances involved.
- o No professional, psychological, or medical advice is implied, stated, or offered in any way whatsoever. You are encouraged to seek professional help, education, advice, and counsel from individuals you deem competent should you desire to learn more about faith, commitments, and spiritual journeys.

- o   Note: certain names and related circumstances may have been changed to protect confidentiality. All stories where names are mentioned are used with the permission of the parties involved, if applicable. Any resemblance to past or current people, places, circumstances, or events is purely coincidental.

Scripture:
- o   All Scripture references are quoted from the New International Version (NIV) of the Holy Bible, unless otherwise noted. **New International Version (NIV) Copyright © 1973, 1978, 1984, 2011 by Biblica**

Website Design: Judy Bowen and Kelly Oberg
www.judy-bowen.com
www.kjopublicrelations.com
Cover design: Justin Aubrey

ISBN 978-1-7350189-3-5

PUBLISHED BY CREATIVE TEAM PUBLISHING
www.CreativeTeamPublishing.com
Ft. Worth, Texas
Printed in the United States of America

Riding the Fence Really Hurts!

Embrace GOD'S Plan for Your Life

Judy Bowen

Dedication

I wish to dedicate this book to these special people:

1. To my amazing parents, Ann and Jack Farr
2. My wonderful, supportive husband, Gary Bowen
3. My big brothers Jack and Ron Farr
4. My loving children and grandchildren: Matt, Abby, Brei, Axis, Paige, Nicole, Matthew, Brycen, and Millie (Amelia).

~Judy Bowen, July, 2021

Table of Contents

Dedication by Judy Bowen   7

Foreword: Dr. Jim Garlow
    www.WellVersedWorld.org   13

Introduction   15

Chapter One
    Daddy's Petunia   17

Chapter Two
    California, Here I Come…   23

Chapter Three
    The First Baptist Church of Clairemont   31

Chapter Four
    The Teen Years and Ugly Thirteen!   35

Chapter Five
    Baptist Camp Life   41

Chapter Six
    Married Life   47

Table of Contents

Chapter Seven
    Just the Two of Us Against the World—
        Could We Make It on Our Own?   *55*

Chapter Eight
    Back on the Fence and "I do" ... Again!   *63*

Chapter Nine
    In and Out of the Cage   *73*

Chapter Ten
    Okay, Satan, Let's Dance!   *79*

Chapter Eleven
    New Job, New Loves, New Life   *85*

Chapter Twelve
    Cowboys, Rodeos, and Radio   *95*

Chapter Thirteen
    The Balancing Act—Diamonds and a Mustang   *107*

Chapter Fourteen
    Vons Grocery Store, and Dimples   *115*

Chapter Fifteen
    Getting to Know You—
        Getting to Know *All* about You!   *123*

Table of Contents

Chapter Sixteen
    Surprise, Surprise, Surprise!   *131*

Chapter Seventeen
    Growing Pains   *143*

Chapter Eighteen
    Biker Bars, Bible Studies, and Building   *153*

Chapter Nineteen
    Okay, Now What?   *161*

Chapter Twenty
    Building a Legacy   *171*

Your Invitation   *183*

*****

PHOTO GALLERY   *185*

CLOSING THOUGHTS   *189*

ABOUT THE AUTHOR   *191*

RESOURCES   *193*

Table of Contents

PRODUCTS AND SERVICES   197

ENDORSEMENTS
 Brian Carlin, Best-Selling Author   199
 The Publisher's Endorsement   201

THE PUBLISHER   203

*****

FOREWORD

Dr. Jim Garlow, www.WellVersedWorld.org

San Diego is blessed with solid, spiritual mentors in church leadership ministries and lay leadership. One of those influencers in leadership and women's counseling is Judy Bowen. Judy is a former radio account executive of KGB radio, a National Sales Manager of KFMB radio and General Manager of Salem Radio Stations; then Marketing and Communications director for The Rock Church, San Diego.

Judy, and her husband, Gary, have been integral in projecting a vibrant Christian faith for years. But that faith has not developed apart from a story of true vulnerability and life-changing mistakes. As Judy says, she was "riding a fence" for a long time, with one foot anchored in God's grace, redemptive hope, and God's unfailing love and forgiveness, and the other foot in the fascination and momentary charms of pursuits away from God; never "leaving" her faith, but decidedly not positioned where she knew God wanted her. She was a prodigal daughter, who ran from but eventually returned to the Father.

Judy's life lessons resonate with blatant truth. No cover-ups; rather, full disclosure including severe pains and griefs.

Foreword

Her story ends with eventually allowing God complete control. She got off of her fence, and left it permanently.

This story doesn't gloss over life's struggles, temptations, failures, and sin. Indeed, her tale includes these mistakes and tells how God continually loved and pursued her in spite of her choices of a life away from Him.

Enjoy and be challenged by a story that will resonate with you and many others because it represents the experiences of many: called by God, struggling in an unyielding posture, returning to the fold, and always forgiven completely. Perfection was not the goal; nor is it ever. Willing submission to her Lord's leading is the goal, and now forever will be her course. She counsels women often because "she's been there." You will read a life history of unvarnished truth.

~ Dr. Jim Garlow 2021

Introduction

The idea for this book and its title, ***Riding the Fence Really Hurts,*** came to me in 2006. I had started teaching a women's Bible study group in my home for the Rock Church here in San Diego. I had also finished my certification through the American Association of Christian Counselors, and was certified as a Biblical Counselor.

I knew from my own life experience and counseling others, that trying to please God and please the world at the same time always ends in pain. Thus, the title.

I wrote two paragraphs and decided I wasn't a writer, didn't have the time, and maybe someday would get back to completing this book. So, my initial writing sat in my "documents" folder on my computer until 2021, for fifteen years! God's timing!

Being retired with fifteen years of teaching the Bible, counseling others, and with numerous life experiences under my belt, I knew this was the right time to finish the book. I had no idea how many people were suffering from "riding the fence."

It seemed everyone I counseled was having the same or a similar challenge, wanting God to bless their lives and wanting to live for Him, but not desiring to be fully obedient to His Word. They wanted God to bless what they wanted and prayed for, selectively picking and choosing what to obey. All the time they were wondering why their lives were a mess and God wasn't showering them with blessings.

The content of the book is my personal autobiography, explaining my on-again, off-again ride on the fence; all the while loving Christ and wanting to please Him, but also yearning to do my own thing. I was asking Him to follow me, instead of me letting Him lead.

I pray you will relate to my story and that it will help you choose to get off the fence and do things God's way, the best way!

I've fully embraced this verse for my life:

Proverbs 3:5 and 6 (NIV)

> [5] Trust in the LORD with all your heart and lean not on your own understanding; [6] in all your ways submit to him, and he will make your paths straight.

Chapter One
Daddy's Petunia

I couldn't help but think of my past eighteen years since birth and the warm hugs while sitting on my daddy's lap as he stroked my hair, kissed my cheek, and called me his "Petunia." I recalled that broad grin on his face as he watched me dance around the room, telling me I could be anything I wanted to be, even a ballerina or a tight rope walker, since I loved watching the girls up on the wire and swinging so high above the awestruck crowd.

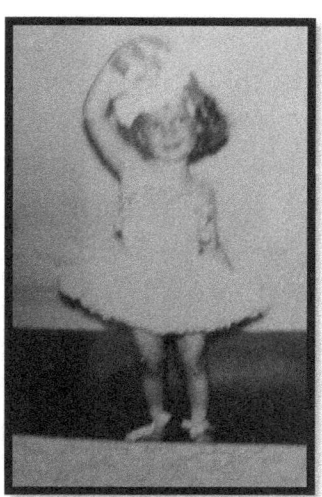

"Daddy's Petunia": Judy's first dance performance, age 3.
The photographer is her father.

But now at eighteen years old, I felt I was all grown up and ready for marriage, just like my mom had been when she married my dad at eighteen.

Judy at age 17, 1969, and how she looked just before she married.
Yearbook photo (1969) taken by Class photographer

Both dad and my fiancé were twenty-one when they married. This wedding day was supposed to be one of the happiest days of my life. But I was hanging on to my dad's arm with all my might with tears streaming down my face as I walked down the isle of our small church, packed with friends and family who had watched our romance blossom over the past three years. I knew in my heart that I was being disobedient to what God was calling me to do, but I was afraid to step away, afraid to disappoint anyone.

Some of the well-respected church goers in our happy little Baptist church would say, "This is a match made in heaven." When I heard that, I always smiled and tried to look as happy as I could, but deep inside I knew I was in a relationship that was hurtful and selfish. I was marrying a guy that had to have his own way, had grown up with an alcoholic father who had abused his mother, and had never been taught how to respect, let alone love, a woman.

Many times, I had plotted out in my mind how to tell him I didn't want to be with him, but so many times the words got stuck in my throat because he told me he was desperately in love with me and couldn't live without me. I wanted to please him and everyone else that seemed to be living their humdrum lives through us. We were that wonderful couple who sang together as she played the piano, we were the couple that led the children's choir and taught Sunday school. We were the couple who had the "perfect" relationship. So, I reasoned and questioned, "How could I let them all down?" My mom's words rang in my ear: "He is not your father; he has no compassion. I give this marriage five years, max!"

Well, my husband and I divorced four years later, our son was two years old, I was twenty-two years old, and a single mom. I got out of the marriage the only way I felt I could by having an affair, seeking love and compassion outside of my marriage and remembering my husband telling me that the only way we would ever get divorced is if adultery is committed, because that is Biblical! This from a man that stole my virginity against my will and wanted me to drop out of school and marry him at sixteen years old so he could have sex anytime he wanted and I couldn't resist! I learned from my years with him what it meant to be "controlled" and afraid to speak up. These were life lessons that served me well in the years to come as I would counsel many women in the same situation.

I was raised in a sheltered "Father Knows Best" family. My dad was a WWII vet, a gunner on a B-29. Thank God he made it home unharmed! My mom was a homemaker. I have two older brothers, nine and five years older than me, respectively. I was born in 1951 in "Philly" after the war, and I was a "surprise" gift to my mom and dad … a girl!

From day one I was cherished. My grandfather's string band even serenaded my mom and me under her hospital window with "Daddy's Little Girl," a popular song at that time. I was performing in dance shows at three years of age to the glee of my dad who laughed the hardest out in the audience since each of us on stage was doing something different. I loved being the center of attention and every Saturday night we would have a jam session at my grandparent's home. My grandmother would play the piano, my "Pop Pop" the electric mandolin, we kids would sing, dance, and perform all to the applause of doting parents and grandparents.

Life was loving, safe, and a cocoon of sorts. 'Seems nothing could ever get in to harm us and I had *no* idea what the "world" had to offer, how the "other half" lived. My life consisted of God, family, laughter, and a lot of love, and I thought it was the same for every child.

Judy's parents, John C. Farr, Jr. and Anna Elizabeth Storm, on their wedding day: June 7, 1941

Chapter Two
CALIFORNIA, HERE I COME...

My dad was tired of shoveling snow every winter in Philadelphia, where my family originates and, in October, 1959, decided to move us to sunny, safe, quiet, San Diego, California. It was heartbreaking leaving my grandparents and our lives together, but my dad was determined to give us a better life. Our journey began in a 1956 Ford sedan with three kids and our dog, Duchess, in the back landing of the car. We sold everything we had, furniture, beds TV, etc. My dad bought a small trailer and only "needed" household items were towed. I was so thankful that my new green bike from Santa had made the cut. My brothers' old bikes did not!

Dad had prepared quite a journey across the U.S., with frequent stops for running up hills and throwing the football around, including stopping in an old western town in Oklahoma to ride on our first horses. My mom would prepare sandwiches as we drove, singing, "California, Here I Come" at least 100 times. (I know I asked 200 times, "When are we going to be there?") and we would sneak a Sterno Canned Heat stove (along with Duchess) into a roadside motel each night to fix dinner.

Judy Bowen

It took nine days to arrive in San Diego. I was eight, my brothers thirteen and eighteen years of age.

We all took to the sunshine, the palm trees, the beach, and outdoor schools; however, mom cried every day and missed her life, family and friends back home. We rented a furnished two-bedroom duplex just up the street from my elementary school. I walked to school and came home for lunch every day. Mom finally made some friends with neighbors and it seemed everyone was a transplant from back east: the Ladd's from Rhode Island, the Stiles family from New York.

Mom loved to entertain and enjoyed having them over as often as possible. My oldest brother, Jack, was a senior in high school when we moved to San Diego; it wasn't easy for him, or my brother, Ron, who was starting Junior High at his new school and being teased for being chubby. I remember him crying and not wanting to go to school.

I, too, was struggling in my new third grade class. I could barely read and the other kids seemed so much smarter. My teacher, Mrs. Hudson, picked up on it right away and spoke to my parents about starting with first-grade books and working my way up to the third-grade level. My dad worked with me every night on my reading and also with flash cards to learn my multiplication tables. A few months in, I was reading to the class and a whiz at the multiplication tables! I was so proud!

Riding the Fence Really Hurts!

We only had to spend six months in that tiny, crowded duplex before my parents found a great house for $15,500.00, on a canyon lot, in a cul-de-sac where *many* tag football games would be played. Jack was the quarterback, Ron and I running backs, and receivers. I loved it! I was a good receiver and with a helmet (required by mom) on my head, begged to play. My brothers would allow it as long as I didn't drop the ball or cry to mom when I got hurt. I still have the scarred knees to show for it ... playing on black top was rough!

To this day football is my favorite sport. It certainly was my dad's and I loved watching the games with him and learning all the rules. The house had 1½ bathrooms and was all one-story. Our "row house" in Philly was three-story with only one bathroom, so my mom was thrilled that her and dad had their own bathroom right off their bedroom. She scrubbed the house from top to bottom and started decorating. Green and blue shag carpet, vein mirrored wall in the living room and, wait for it ... an eight-foot, yellow Naugahyde couch! Yep, we were now into the 60s! Groovy baby!

My brothers both settled into their schools and did well. Jack graduated high school in the summer of 1960 and found a job up the street at Oscar's car hop restaurant, where you would sit in your car and the cute waitresses would bring your food to your car. All the high school kids would hang out there, listening to music, and drinking cokes. Jack was a busboy and could eat all he wanted! I thought that was so groovy and loved walking up to Oscar's with my little friend to see my big brother. Junior hot fudge sundaes were only 25 cents, loaded with whip crème and nuts, and we were hooked!

Ron made some nice friends at school, graduated Junior High, and went on to high school where he tried out for football, played in a band, and sang. I had started taking piano lessons at age twelve, and was so proud that I could teach him chords on the keyboard that he played in the band! To me, he was a rock star!

My dad bought an old speed boat and we all learned to ski in the San Diego Bay. All but mom: she continued to cook on the Sterno stove and would make sloppy Joes at the bay! New friends would join in and at the end of the day mom's favorite thing was cruising slowly on the bay, with the lights lit on the boat at sunset, in the calm waters. We were creating new "San Diego memories" and my dad beamed with pride that his vision and dream for us was unfolding. We had made the move and had settled into our new lives. Mom, too, beamed; and although many homesick tears had been shed, she supported, trusted, and loved my dad and would follow him to the ends of the earth if he thought that would be best for us all. Their love and respect for each other was the stuff fairy tales were made of, and what I wanted so desperately in my life.

Riding the Fence Really Hurts!

My brothers found love and both married when they were twenty-one, and are still married to their first loves, following in my parent's footsteps. Who would have ever guessed I would be the black sheep of the family?

(Left to Right) Ron, Judy, and Jack
1956

Judy Bowen

Ready for Football in Philadelphia:
(Left to right) Ron, Judy (with helmet) and Jack
1958

Riding the Fence Really Hurts!

A Golden Wedding Anniversary

Jack and Ann (parents) in front; Judy, Jack, and Ron in the back, on occasion of the parents' 50th Wedding Anniversary, June 7, 1991.

Chapter Three
THE FIRST BAPTIST CHURCH OF CLAIREMONT

After arriving in San Diego my parents knew it was important to find a local church. We attended a Protestant church in Philly, so we visited the local one a few times and didn't feel it was a fit. We were then invited to a little Baptist church, also in the neighborhood, and we liked the friendly pastor and welcoming parishioners. It was a Bible-teaching, close-knit congregation with frequent potlucks (my mom loved that), junior church for younger kids that included a junior choir (I loved that), and we felt right at home.

More interesting and strange to me was a big "baptismal" pool behind the stage where the pastor would totally submerge new believers after their confession of faith in Jesus as the Son of God who forgave their sins. This was done, I was taught, because this was the way Jesus was baptized and we were to follow His example. But, before you could be baptized you had to accept Jesus into your heart by publicly professing your faith in Christ by walking down the aisle, after a sermon, up to the pastor, who would welcome you into the family of believers, and everyone would cheer and clap.

Every sermon ended with an invitation to come forward and accept Jesus as your Lord and Savior. It was my favorite part of the service, and even if I had fallen asleep on my mom's shoulder, I would wake up for this and I would feel *so* happy for those people.

It didn't take long for my nine-year-old little heart to be beating out of my chest as I too felt the tug on my heart to take that walk down the aisle and ask Jesus into my heart as my Lord and Savior. My mom and dad moved out of the pew so I could get by, and I walked all by myself into the sweet arms of my pastor and Jesus! O Happy Day! Yes, everyone clapped and cheered, my parents cried, and I was so happy I could have burst! My parents decided to officially join the church and walk forward, as did my brothers. We were baptized as a family in that "pool behind the stage," one at a time. I was the last to get dunked and came out of that water with more joy than I could explain.

My grandparents gave me a little white Bible that had some blank pages in the back of it. I started writing love poems to Jesus, telling Him how much I loved Him. I knew I would always belong to Him and He would always love and protect me, just like my earthly father had done. That church was a huge part of our lives. My faith grew as I learned scripture and shared during Sunday School. My dad taught Junior High Sunday school and became a deacon, my mom a deaconess. We had lovely friends that we became close to. We would go to Sunday school and church in the morning,

Riding the Fence Really Hurts!

and then back for evening services, and on Wednesdays, prayer meetings and potlucks. There were always kids' services and high school programs like BYF (Baptist Youth Fellowship) as I got older. As my piano lessons continued, I was asked to play the piano at the casual Sunday night services.

Sunday night worship was a "request a song" time. If someone requested a song that was too complicated for me, I would tell them, "Sorry, pick another one," and everyone would laugh and chose something else. I was encouraged and hugged a lot!

> I knew I would always belong to Him and He would always love and protect me, just like my earthly father had done.

Chapter Four
THE TEEN YEARS AND UGLY THIRTEEN!

My thirteenth birthday came and just like that, I was a teenager! Junior High School, new friends, begging my mom to shave my legs, becoming a "woman," finally the sign of boobs, and boys! But thirteen would not be a cake walk and would test my faith at an early age. The number 13, known as a bad luck number, certainly didn't disappoint ... ugh!

After several sore throats it was decided my tonsils and adenoids needed to come out. Ouch! The Jell-O and ice cream was nice! Next there was a tooth growing through the roof of my mouth (I was told I had a very small mouth ... my brothers didn't' agree) that needed to be dug out. Ouch! Oh, so much blood; my dad, who was there for moral support, had to leave the room or potentially faint!

Our neighborhood was filled with canyons and one had a train track at the bottom. My girlfriends and I decided to climb down to walk on the oily train tracks, I lost my balance, slipped and fell on the track and cracked my pelvis. I still had to climb back up the canyon to get out. Ouch! I didn't tell my mom at first and then had to confess because the pain was bad.

This next one was the strangest and scariest. Not being accustomed to growing breasts, I realized my right one was growing larger than my left. I sought counsel with my other thirteen-year-old girlfriends and we agreed that was probably normal. However, I also noticed it was very hard, unlike my normal squishy left breast. So, I decided to tell mom and of course she wanted to see and touch (so embarrassing) and immediately knew something wasn't right.

The doctor confirmed that I had a baseball size tumor growing and it had to come out right away and most likely could be cancer due to the size and how long it had been growing. I went into the hospital the next day. But when I came home from the doctor, I found comfort and peace in playing those hymns I had played in church on my piano. A calm came over me and I could feel Jesus holding my hand, holding me close, and telling me He was with me, and all would be fine. My mom later told me that she and my dad couldn't sleep and prayed and cried all night. The tumor came out, benign, no cancer (they had prepped me for a full hysterectomy); I had no pain, and came home in a couple of days. No "ouch" this time, only a grateful, thankful heart, knowing my heavenly Father was faithful and "would never leave me or forsake me," and I could trust Him with my life!

Riding the Fence Really Hurts!

> A calm came over me and I could feel Jesus holding my hand, holding me close, and telling me He was with me, and all would be fine.

Finally, my 13th year of bad luck ended as soon as summer started, or so I thought, and we were all *so* happy to be back at the beach, sharing food and cokes, swimming, and surfing. I soon started to feel weak and sick and was diagnosed with Mono (mononucleosis), the "kissing disease!" I had to convince my mom and dad it wasn't from kissing boys; but from sharing cokes, and I spent the rest of the summer in bed, too tired to do anything. Final Ouch! I could hardly wait for my 14th birthday in August! Good-bye, 13!

I loved Junior High school! Changing classrooms, passing notes in the hallway, changing into our gym clothes for P.E. (Physical Education) So many new friends, slumber parties, and baby doll pajamas, and so many cute boys! I had a new boyfriend weekly; I just couldn't decide, and experienced my first kiss. There were school dances and on rainy days we stayed in the gym to square dance. I seemed to always get paired up with the guy with sweaty palms and two left feet that were most of the time treading on mine!

But my favorite class was choir! All the singing I had done growing up, with my family and at church, along with piano lessons that allowed me to read music, gave me confidence and I caught onto the alto parts of the songs with ease. And, of course, there were the performances in front of the school and parents. I was so proud and loved performing.

My soon-to-be best friend arrived at the school in the 8th grade; they had moved to San Diego from Washington D.C., another transplant from the east coast. Jackie was cute and super smart, laughed really loud, and loved to sing. We would spend hours with me playing piano and her singing at the top of her lungs in our living room. She was the oldest of seven children and their home was like a circus, kids literally bouncing off the walls. Of course, all the neighbor kids would come to hang out there and the real draw was their pool! How no one ever drowned is a miracle!

Her mom had the patience of a saint, her dad, not so much. Her mom would line up the seven kids for dinner and each would hold out their plate for food. There were times when a neighbor would fall into line and one of her own kids missed out. She would tell them to go make a peanut butter sandwich and make sure the neighbors were gone home at dinner time, because once she counted seven kids, the food was gone!

Because of the chaos in their three-bedroom home, Jackie would beg to stay at my house where there was peace and quiet and plenty of food. Sometimes she would wake me up at midnight after my parents had gone to bed and ask if she could have salad with French dressing. I always said yes and would watch her devour a big bowl. I loved her like a sister and wanted to take care of her. I always had to remind her to use her quiet voice when she came over and not to use the word "bitchen." My mom hated that word and couldn't understand why it described just about everything! When our year books were signed by all our friends, that word was all over the place and my mom was horrified. I never wanted her to read what the other kids wrote. I never used the word in front of my parents out of respect. I always wanted to be the good Christian girl that they were proud of and bragged about. They deserved that for being such wonderful parents.

Jackie was being raised Catholic and would try to explain her religion to me. It sounded so different from my Baptist, Christian upbringing. Her parents didn't take their children to church but they all had been through Catechism classes; however, she knew very little about the Bible and a loving Jesus that loved her and died for her and rose again! I shared my faith with her and Bible verses and stories about Jesus. She came to church with me and was getting very excited about Christianity and living for Jesus. She saw my love for Jesus and told me she wanted to accept Jesus as her Savior!

My heart was so full and we cried and laughed and swore we would live our lives for Jesus and tell others about Him. When she told her dad, he picked her up and threw her against the wall for denouncing the Catholic religion. He wanted nothing to do with her new beliefs. Her persecution at home began, but she stayed strong and she and I would enter into high school sharing the Four Spiritual Laws (a pamphlet on how to become a Christian) with everyone that would listen. We were active in Campus Life, a Christian organization for high school kids, we had Bible studies in my home, went to retreats with other Christian kids, and our faith grew! I had a true sister in Christ!

Chapter Five
Baptist Camp Life

Entering high school was exciting and scary! We had left Junior High at the top of the food chain and now were entering the hallowed halls of Madison High School at the bottom. Us newbies would huddle together in the morning before school and at lunch, hoping we would be placed in some classes together for moral support. I continued singing in the choir and eventually tried out for the elite acapella Madrigal group with only twelve members. I was accepted as an alto and once again, leaning on my piano music lessons, could easily read music. There were competitions against other schools that we would all travel to, and trophies!

I also jumped with both feet into the drama program, and this class was more fun than I could have ever imagined. My favorite was improv and the crazy story lines we would come up with. Of course, this allowed me to be back onstage doing plays, singing, while enjoying the clapping and cheers of the audience. My mind began to wander, and I wondered if this could be my future, something I could be successful at as my career? I would watch musicals with actresses that sang and danced and would imagine myself in their roles.

It seemed that my life up to this point had led in this direction, but doubts of not being talented enough also entered into my mind. I asked God for direction and that I would please Him in whatever He had planned for me.

Now in high school, I would be eligible to attend Baptist Winter Camp! It was way up in the mountains at Camp Palomar. We always prayed for snow and wondered if there would be cute boys from the other Baptist churches who would attend. The gals would stay in wooden cabins with our camp counselors (women from our church who volunteered) and the boys stayed in old Quonset huts made of aluminum from WW II.

The mission was for us gals to sneak out at night and toilet paper the boy's huts, then take our counselors girdle and hoist it up the flag pole! Mission accomplished, and we were so proud of ourselves, and *so* blessed we had a fun-loving counselor, Ethel, who laughed at seeing her girdle waving in the air when we all went down to the chow hall for breakfast.

There would be lots of noise and laughter as we filled up on oatmeal, pancakes, and hot chocolate, then would come the dreaded "announcements" for the day. At once a chorus of "announcements, announcements, announcements, a terrible death to die, a terrible death to die, a terrible death to be talked to death, a terrible death to die, announcements, announcements, announcements" would ensue. This would

Riding the Fence Really Hurts!

continue each time the director would try to speak until we were sternly told to quiet down!

Us gals continued to scout for cute boys from other churches who might be looking our way. And then it happened: a cute boy approached me from the Baptist church downtown. His sidekick, not so cute. He had a huge smile and was full of energy as he told me his name and that he was a senior in high school (I was a sophomore) and had a car and wondered if he could walk with me on the upcoming hike. I agreed … why, oh why, did I agree? My girlfriends exited stage right and there I was alone with "Mr. Happy," sticking to me like glue for the rest of the retreat weekend. I wanted to be having fun with my friends and to tell him to give me some space, but didn't want to be rude and he was *so* aggressively pursuing me, which made a fifteen-year-old Judy feel pretty special. But all too soon he was trying to kiss me, and very handsy on the hike as it started to get dark. "What was happening and how do I handle this as a naive fifteen years old?" My ego told me to be flattered that an eighteen-year-old boy liked me, but my Christian upbringing and love for Jesus told me, "Something's wrong with this picture!"

He took my number and as soon as I arrived back home, the phone started to ring. He wanted to drive to my house and meet me and my parents, and go out. I told my folks about meeting him at camp and they were happy we met at a Christian camp, thinking he was a respectable, good, Christian boy with good intentions. I also told them he was a senior in high school and eighteen years old. That was the same age my dad was when he met my fifteen-year-old mom at the community pool in Philly. They dated three years and married. That piece of information made them have second thoughts. Was I old enough to date a boy much older and with a car? I knew once he met them with his big smile and outgoing personality, he would win them over. Inside my head I was screaming, "Mom, Dad, I'm not ready for this; please say, 'No.'" My first "ride on the fence" began as they agreed that "he was such a polite young man with good intentions" that I could date him. This was January, 1967, just four months into my high school years.

It became clear early on that he didn't want to share me with my friends, and anytime I would try to explain I was going to hang out with them instead of him, he would become sullen and jealous asking why didn't I want to spend time with him? "Who was more important, my friends, or him?" I would always cave and give in to him and let my friends go on without me, knowing I was missing out and realizing they soon would stop asking me to join them. Even my best friend, Jackie, started doing things without me or with her boyfriend who lived in the neighborhood and was our age.

I felt lonely and isolated. Now my entire life revolved around this guy and his agenda … *sex*! His car became a prison and his advances were non-stop regardless of my constant expressions of "No!" He would tell me, "It's okay: we love each other and we're going to get married." Love, marriage, are you kidding me? I'm fifteen and I want to have fun with my friends, go to dances and football games, sing, act, go the beach, attend Campus Life meetings and Bible studies, and be the good little Christian girl I was raised to be. He was relentless and I held him off thinking he would tire of it and find someone else to harass.

When I turned sixteen, he decided I should drop out of school and get my parent's permission to marry, knowing this would be the answer to my "No's." I remember him turning his car radio all the way up as the Beatles song "All You Need is Love" was playing and I was walking away into my house. I told him there was no way my parents would agree to that and that I couldn't, either.

This was the perfect time to "jump off the fence" that was unbearable, and choose to go on with my dreams, God's plan, my life! But, once again, he pleaded that he needed me, said all the right things, gave me a 45-rpm record "You're Just Too Good to Be True," and I stayed. He forced me soon after that to "give in." I cried and asked God to forgive me and told myself that now I had to marry him. That was a lie from the pit of hell!

> [9] If we confess our sins, he is faithful and just and will forgive us our sins and purify us from all unrighteousness. 1 John 1:9 (NIV)

Judy Bowen

My parents would never find out I was not a virgin when I married. This was a secret well-kept which ate at me, knowing I had lied to them.

I was thankful to still have my best friend, Jackie, and she and I would talk in depth about all of this. She, too, had found an older guy, with a car, and they were having sex and she, too, was feeling the guilt and shame. She had the courage to leave that relationship. She encouraged me to do the same. Her dreams of college and mission work were strong, and she graduated high school with honors and went off to Chattanooga Tennessee Temple College, met a wonderful Christian guy, and married. I left my dreams behind, too afraid to speak up, and walked down the aisle on my wedding day, crying.

One of my biggest regrets to this very day is that Jackie and I lost touch with each other when my husband dragged me and our one-year-old son off to Brownwood, Texas, to go to the university there. He had decided he wanted to be a minister! I've tried for years to find Jackie, but never have been successful. It still brings me to tears, and I still miss her.

Chapter Six
MARRIED LIFE

Right after graduation from high school, at age seventeen, I immediately went to work, 40 hours a week at the bank up the street from our home. My dad was friends with the manager and got me the job. My "new" goal was to save money that we would need once we were married seven months later. I was so proud: I had saved $1,000!

I remember lying in bed on my wedding night crying because I missed my parents, the safety of our home, and my cute bedroom that mom had decorated while I was away at a retreat. I pulled myself together with these words: "This was my life now, grow up and get used to it."

The Vietnam war was in full swing and my new husband was in college (or so I thought) trying to avoid being drafted. We had been married six months. I was working hard, coming home, fixing dinner, and constantly cleaning up as he was like a tornado when he walked in the door. His mom had picked up after him his entire life, and now it was my job.

He soon received a notice in the mail that he had been drafted. I then found out he was not attending school, but out playing golf with friends! He went off to boot camp, I moved back in with my folks, and six weeks later we were stationed at Fort Sam Houston in San Antonio, Texas. This would be my first time living away from home.

I had prayed that he would not be sent to Vietnam, and once again God was my faithful Father, and answered that prayer. My husband was assigned to a small annex that housed the officers and was given the position of "Colonels Aid." His duties consisted of taking the officers children to school and picking them up, picking up dignitaries who would come into town, and when things were slow, fishing in the stocked ponds on the premise. A long cry from going to Vietnam! Thank you, Jesus!

We had purchased a 12x56 mobile home and parked it in a family friendly mobile home park. It had orange shag carpet and black fake leather furniture, so ugly! We joined the First Baptist church of San Antonio and got involved with the youth group and choir. Life was good for us in San Antonio and people were open and friendly, and readily invited us over for "BBQ" after just meeting us. It was also good for us to be making it on our own, away from family, forced to grow up. Although, my parents, my sister-in-law and her two kids, ages four years and fifteen months all came to visit in the summer and stayed with us for a week! I thought my dad would pass out in the humid, God-awful heat. He spent most of his time laying across an air conditioning vent on the floor.

Riding the Fence Really Hurts!

When they left, I cried and longed to be back in San Diego with them.

It didn't take long for my wish to come true. The war ended and we got an "early out" from the army. We had only been in for fifteen months. When we got back to San Diego we stayed with my folks for a while, and would soon find out that I was with child. I had told my husband I felt certain I was pregnant and asked him if he wanted to come to the appointment with me. He told me he would rather my mom go and he needed his sleep, it was a morning appointment. When the pregnancy was confirmed at the doctor's office, I was excited to get back to tell him about it. He was still in bed when I arrived and I woke him to tell him the exciting news; his response? "Oh, that's just great timing, me out of work and you pregnant and no insurance now that we're out of the Army." He then put the pillow over his head and went back to sleep. My mom was livid! I was hurt and afraid of what kind of father he would be, and cried ... again.

My husband was thrilled after my 48 hours in labor (he went home to sleep, of course), and an emergency C section were over. I gave birth to a healthy, beautiful baby boy. Our son was to be named Andrew, one of my favorite names, but right before we were to give the hospital his name, in true "controlling" fashion, my husband decided he should be Matthew. I was too tired to argue, and Matthew means "gift from God," so I was good with the name. My Matthew has truly been a gift from God, and now I know God named him.

He now has a son also named Matthew. God continues to be a faithful, loving Father!

As expected, my husband had no idea how to be a good father. His father was certainly not a good example for him. He was a self-centered alcoholic with no respect for his loving wife or children. I remember his mom telling me, "Just love him, love him." That's what she had done throughout her marriage, regardless of the way she was treated or the way he treated their children. This advice made me sick to my stomach, and I would not stand by and watch a father that would spank his one-year-old son for crying when he was sick or wanting to be held and cuddled. It broke my heart and broke apart any little bit of love I had left for my husband, now a controlling father. I had to get out for Matthew's sake and my own. I wouldn't ride this fence any longer; the pain was getting worse.

Matthew was two years old; we'd been living in the tiny town of Brownwood almost a year. I had been leading a high school group of gals at our church, directing the children's choir, and trying to stay busy. The pay was so poor at the bank that it wasn't worth it to pay for child care and to go to work. We were so poor, living by the skin of our teeth, God's grace, and the kindness of others. My life consisted of riding a bike with Matthew on the back, window shopping at Woolworths, cleaning the house daily to keep up with my husband's messes, going to church, and watching soap operas.

Riding the Fence Really Hurts!

I heard about a local civic theatre group that was auditioning for a play and would be presenting a dinner theatre experience for the town. I auditioned and was given the lead role. I was ecstatic! Back on the stage! Enter, stage left, the President of the theatre group. A tall, Greek God-looking man, who was the history professor at the college. My jaw dropped and I was smitten. How could anyone be that handsome, smart, and engaging. I was once again back on that uncomfortable fence! He too was immediately drawn to me and the rest is history!

The dinner theatre was a success. Being back on the stage to cheering and clapping was exhilarating, but not as exciting as the forbidden fruit. The affair would last only a month before my husband would become a detective and follow me and discover the truth. He destroyed the professor's career and also his marriage, calling his wife and telling her everything. I learned later, disgraced, they had to move out of town. I called and confessed to my parents. They sent me a plane ticket, and I returned home with Matthew, to the only real home I'd ever known, back to the safety of my father's arms. My husband packed up what was left, after destroying all my favorite albums, and moved back in with his parents in San Diego.

The big question now was whether to divorce or not divorce. I knew I wanted out but thought it only fair to hear him out. He came over to my parents' home while they were out. Matthew, now two, was napping. My stomach was in knots when he walked in. I knew his history of sweettalking me into what he wanted, but this time I took control. I told him, "I know I've messed up and have been unfaithful, but I can't go on living the way we have. You have to change and be a better husband and father in order for this to ever work." I already knew what his response would be ... "You're the one that did the unthinkable; there is nothing I need to change. I've done nothing wrong; I don't need to change for anyone." And there it was, the answer I wanted and needed. I felt relief flood my body and told him that wouldn't work for me and that we needed to get divorced and then get on with our lives. He told me I was an unfit mother and he would do everything he could to get Matthew away from me and live with him. This did scare me, but I knew he wouldn't follow through; he didn't want to take care of Matthew. He was too self-centered and self-absorbed.

He asked if he could go in and look at Matthew as he was sleeping before he left. I agreed and then he pinned me against the wall in the hallway, his arms on either side of me and said, "We're still married and you're still my wife. I want to have sex!" I felt a rush of anger, remembering *all* the times I was "required" to have sex with him, regardless of how I felt, the years flashing in my mind of feeling helpless and out of control. I pushed him off me and told him to get out. He did.

We had no assets so we did a "do-it-yourself" type divorce. He eventually moved to another city about 600 miles

Riding the Fence Really Hurts!

north of San Diego and rarely checked in on Matthew. I found a low-income apartment for Matthew and me to live in, and went to work at another bank in San Diego. Matthew went into daycare. My parents continued to be my support, always willing to help whenever needed. My brothers, too, were always there for me, helping me move into my apartment, inviting us over for dinner, playing volleyball on the weekends, checking in on their little sister. I was so grateful for my family.

Chapter 7
JUST THE TWO OF US AGAINST THE WORLD— COULD WE MAKE IT ON OUR OWN?

It was 1974 and the popular song, "You and Me Against the World," by Helen Reddy, had just been released. Matthew and I had moved into our own place, a two-bedroom, low rent apartment on the third floor. I made it a home for us, even with the donated furniture from my folks and brother that I was so grateful for. Finally, there was no one to answer to, to clean up after, and no more feeling trapped. It was the freedom I had longed for. I could hold and love on Matthew without being told to "just let him cry." It was the first time I had truly been on my own since I had left my parents' home and married. Could I be content without a man? Could we make it on our own?

I reached out to some friends from high school who had been involved with music. One gal in particular sang a duet with me at one of the school shows.

She was now singing with a band. She invited me out to one of her gigs on a boat cruise around San Diego Harbor. I had never been to a club or been a part of that scene. Never had an alcoholic drink, smoked a cigarette, smoked weed, cursed ... nada! She assured me I would have fun dancing; I did love to dance and hadn't done that in many years.

The rain started coming down and the gig on the boat was cancelled. However, that didn't deter Debbie; she insisted we still go out dancing down in Pacific Beach at a local dance club with the look and feel of a "saloon." A saloon? "Are you crazy?" I asked. "What do you do there, what do I wear, what will I drink, I will feel so out of place, and would God approve?" She reassured me that she would be there with me to enjoy the music, dance some, have some fun, and that I needed to get out.

My wardrobe was very limited. I hadn't bought anything new in quite some time; there was no money for that. I would have to make do with what I had. I pulled on a high neck sweater and some slacks. My folks would babysit Matthew at their house (they had a crib there and he would stay there often.) They spoiled him, which he needed, and loved him so very much. My dad would become the father figure in Matthew's life. What a true blessing from God!

Debbie picked me up and we were off. My stomach was in knots as we arrived at this local night club, showed our IDs, (glad I remembered my license), and entered into a smokey, loud, crowded, big, stinky room with a bar and little tables surrounding the dance floor. Debbie found us a table that would become my safe place, and the cocktail waitress yelled, "What'll you have?" I ordered a 7up ®, Debbie a beer. My 7up came with cherries; that was a nice surprise. We tried to talk in between songs, trying to catch up, but it was easier just to watch the sweaty bodies dancing, drinking, and smoking. So much dancing, drinking and smoking. Some smoke smelled weird to me. I leaned into Debbie and asked, "What is that smell?" I was told it was marijuana. I felt like a little church mouse that was just dropped into a sewer of rats! This was not where I belonged, but I did want to dance and have some fun, and I didn't want to disappoint Debbie.

We hadn't been there too long when we both were asked to dance. Debbie gave me the "go ahead" nod and I followed a cute, very sweaty guy to the dance floor. I had been watching him dance. He was a good dancer and when a song would end, he would want to dance to another, then another, etc., etc. I finally told him I needed to sit down and rest. That 7up with cherries tasted *so* good, and why did I wear a high neck sweater? I, too, was now hot and sweaty. He continued to dance every dance and would glance my way with a "Are you ready to dance again?" smile on his face. I wanted some time at my "safe place" to cool down, and would shake my head, "No."

He asked if he could sit with us and I learned his name was John. He was in the Navy with a few more months left to serve, and he was from Pittsburg. He was very polite and sweet. I told him my name and introduced Debbie. We danced until I was ready to collapse. His energy never seemed to give out. He asked me for my number so I gave him my parents phone number just before we left, never expecting to hear from him or ever see him again.

That was my last trip to a club with Debbie. I just didn't feel comfortable in that environment and my parents agreed. Now that I was on my own and a responsible mother and churchgoing Christian, I believed that I should not be frequenting clubs. I would miss the dancing, though.

I wondered if I would ever meet someone that would want a divorcee with a two-year-old. Satan filled my mind with lies of who I was now, "used goods, an adulteress;" and that even though I was back at church, the church folks, too, knew my story and were looking down on me, gossiping about me, just pretending to be nice and forgiving.

I felt like the woman caught in the act of adultery and thrown down in front of Jesus as her tormentors reminded Jesus of the law that she should be stoned. Ah, but Jesus responds, "Let anyone without sin throw the first stone." When the woman, down on the ground with her head buried in her hands, looked up at Jesus, into those loving, compassionate eyes, He said, "Woman, where are your accusers (for they had all walked away)? Neither do I accuse you. Go and sin no more." Praise God my sins, too, were

Riding the Fence Really Hurts!

forgiven and I was a new creature in Christ as well. I am holy, I am righteous, I am wonderfully redeemed, set apart, with a brand-new heart; I am *free* indeed! "Thank you, Jesus. I'm off the fence and in your comfortable, loving arms. Keep us safe and me focused on *You*!"

> Praise God my sins, too, were forgiven and I was a new creature in Christ as well. I am holy, I am righteous, I am wonderfully redeemed, set apart, with a brand-new heart; I am *free* indeed!

The phone rang and it was mom telling me that a man had called named John, whom I had met when I went out dancing. She said he seemed like a nice enough fellow and she gave him my number. Okay, okay, now what? My heart was pounding, knowing he would call and most likely ask me out. I hadn't dated since I was fifteen and with only one guy, my husband! I decided I would take his call and get more background information on "John." When he called, we talked for quite a while on the phone. He told me he was divorced with two young sons who his wife had taken back to Pittsburg. He told me he missed them terribly. He needed to decide, when he was discharged from the Navy, whether he, too, would move back to Pittsburg or stay in San Diego, which he loved. He was an aircraft electrician on the Naval ship *The USS Hornet* and was five years older than me. I told him I, too, was divorced with a two-year-old son named

Matthew and that I was twenty-three years old. He asked me out. I said, "Yes."

He picked me up at my parents' home; they would be babysitting Matthew. I wanted them to meet him and see who I was going out with. I felt like a teenager again. He arrived right on time, looking handsome and well-dressed, not dripping with sweat like the first time we met. We went to dinner and continued the "getting to know you" process. I was too nervous to eat much and I had an ice tea. He had a beer.

All I could think about was telling him how important my faith was to me and how much I loved Jesus. So, I did. He hung on my every word and told me that he hadn't grown up religious, and that most of his friends growing up were Catholic. His sister, his only sibling, was married to a very devout Catholic who went to church every Sunday; his sister did not attend.

I explained that my relationship with Jesus was not a religion; rather, a way of life, that I followed the scriptures and what Jesus taught, and that I had learned to do this lifestyle growing up in a Baptist church with Christian parents. He took me back to my folks' house and told me he would like to know more about Jesus and hoped we could go out again and talk. That made me very happy. I got a quick peck on the lips and he was off. He was a complete gentleman, not pushy or full of himself. Gentle and kind.

Riding the Fence Really Hurts!

We would spend hours talking about Jesus after that; he had so many questions. He also confessed to me that during the Vietnam war when he was overseas for months, he and his buddies would get high on various drugs they could easily acquire. They would even work while high on the flight deck … dangerous work! He said it was crazy and he was so happy he was getting out and away from all of that. I told him my experience of accepting Christ at nine-years old, getting baptized and sharing my faith all through high school with anyone who would listen.

Boy, did this guy need Jesus! I asked him if he would like to accept Jesus as his Lord and Savior, and with tears swelling up in his eyes, he said, "*Yes!*" I led him in the prayer: "Jesus, I ask you to come into my life. I believe that you love me and died for my sins and that you are the son of God. I confess my sins to you and ask you to forgive me of my sins and cleanse me now and be my Lord and Savior. In Jesus name, Amen." I can truly say that this was and remains one of the most joyous moments of my life, and absolutely the most joyous of John's. It was a turning point in our relationship and I knew that God had brought him into my life.

Chapter 8
BACK ON THE FENCE AND "I DO" ... AGAIN!

After John's conversion, things got hot and heavy. I yearned to be in the loving arms of someone who really cared and was kind and considerate. He was now a Christian and wanted to grow in the Lord! Surely God would overlook our passion and see we were wanting to serve Him and go deeper into our faith.

Back onto the fence I jumped! I was compromising, favoring my needs and desires over God's Word and plan for my life.

John moved into the apartment with Matthew and me. Of course, my parents did not approve or understand how I could do this, but they liked him, and my brothers liked him; my friends, now "our" friends thought he was funny and great.

Matthew, on the other hand, wasn't ready for a new daddy; still, we pushed forward.

Looking back, it was a selfish move on my part. A year after John moved in, we were married by our pastor in the garden behind the little Baptist church ... it was a "family only" event. Both of us were feeling guilty for "living in sin." Matthew was three and a half. I had been single for a year! Now it was back to another man; and yet another fence to hurdle was coming my way.

We were very involved in the new Calvary Chapel meeting in the old North Park Theatre in San Diego. We loved the church and the friends we met there. John was struggling with what to do with his life after serving nine years in the military. He took some classes at City College and got a boring job that he hated. I still worked at the bank and was learning to be a branch specialist, getting proficient at all the different positions in the bank, eventually getting off the teller line and over to the platform side of the bank, opening accounts, interviewing loan customers, and eventually becoming the assistant to the loan officers and bank manager.

John seemed stuck. He was on a roller coaster: happy one day, down the next. I became the cheer leader, always encouraging and reminding him he belonged to Christ and that "... he can do all things through Christ who strengthens him." He had no confidence in himself or his abilities. I could also see from not having his own two sons to father, that Matthew was becoming his anger outlet. John was belittling him and calling him a "mommy's baby." I was constantly stepping in and comforting little Matthew and begging John to let up.

My sister-in-law had a close friend who was a gardener with the city schools. This friend said they were hiring and John applied, and got a job as a gardener. He had no one to really oversee him once he was assigned his schools and knew what to do. He loved that, after being commanded for many years in the Navy. But, even with the new job, the roller coaster of emotions continued.

He finally came clean and told me he was still "using." It was marijuana mostly and now that he basically had no one to answer to at work, he would get high during the day as he worked. He called it the "monkey on his back" that kept jumping back on him from the cage John would regularly put him in. John would stay clean for a couple of months and do well, and then something (the enemy) would trigger him and he would start using again. His ups and downs now began to make sense, along with his off-again on-again ridicule of Matthew.

We talked and talked, and prayed and prayed. I didn't know about AA (Alcoholics Anonymous) meetings, and we were too embarrassed to go to the church for help. We loved each other, stayed involved with the church, and lived for the good times when the monkey stayed in its cage. However, Matthew was still being belittled and it broke my heart.

Judy Bowen

We bought a condo conversion home and got out of the low-income apartments. My dad lent us the down payment. We stayed there two years, and sold it for a nice profit, paid my dad back, and moved into a three-bedroom, two-bath, fixer upper when Matthew was seven. The yard, front and back, was solid gray rocks and the house was painted gray. The back yard was a good size and I begged John to please get rid of the rocks and plant grass. For goodness sakes, he was a gardener! But it was the same story of the cobbler's children not having new shoes. He was too tired to do that once he was home and the *Three Stooges* were on TV.

We did have weekly Bible studies in our home and we loved that, and stayed strong in our beliefs, church ministry, and did our best to get by. John was offered a "head gardener" position, giving him his own crew, but he turned it down several times, not wanting the responsibility. I would continue to climb up the ladder at the bank to make more money.

The big question we had talked about for almost five years was whether to have a child of our own. Matthew was now eight and very independent, playing little league, soccer, riding his bike to school. Did we really want to start over with a baby? Also, John was still paying child support to the mom of the two boys he never saw. It was a heavy burden on his heart.

Riding the Fence Really Hurts!

His two boys came to visit and we told them about Jesus; they both accepted Christ as their Savior and we were both overjoyed. The oldest wanted to come back and live with us, so we agreed. He was hanging with a bad group of kids in Pittsburg and we knew it wouldn't end well if he stayed there. He only lasted with us a couple of weeks, didn't like our rules and lifestyle, and wanted the freedom his mom allowed. He did end up in trouble with the law and has been in and out of prison most of his life; so very sad. He has held onto his faith and leans on it for strength and comfort. He was in his 50s at this writing, and back in prison. John cries over this and feels responsible for not being in his life when he needed him.

One morning John woke up and told me he had dreamt a very vivid dream, which was unusual for him since he never could remember his dreams due to drugs frying parts of his brain. But this dream was like watching a live movie. He was running and playing with a little girl with blonde hair and blue eyes, picking her up and carrying her; she was about three years old. Her name was Abigail/Abby and she was our daughter. About three to four months later I found out I was pregnant and we knew: this child was Abigail.

We looked up her name and story in the Bible and learned she was a wife to King David after her "heart of stone" husband was struck dead by God. She was described as beautiful and intelligent, and David loved her. Needless to say, our Abby was born, blonde and blue eyed, beautiful and intelligent, and "a fathers joy," the meaning of her name. We were the happiest we had ever been; we had been praying this would be a new beginning filled with hope.

Abby was a true delight to us all, even big brother Matthew would bring his friends over to see his new sister; he was so proud. Of course, she became the apple of her Daddy's eye and he cherished her, leaving Matthew feeling like he was the awkward step child even more than he had before. I could see him withdrawing a bit, spending more time out of the house with friends, riding his bike to baseball practice daily, and really embracing the attention of his coaches. They always told me Matt was a team player and a good kid. I attended as many games as I could, as did my dad. John didn't attend many.

John did, on occasion, take Matt out for nature hikes which I encouraged, and Matt seemed to enjoy … I think. Or perhaps he was just trying to make me happy. We always have had a very close, special bond, and he felt like he needed to watch out for me, protect me, and give me lots of hugs. I know that he knew I was doing everything in my power to make sure he was happy and not feeling neglected.

We didn't have money for vacations but when Abby was thirteen months old, and literally running, John's sister and parents planned a vacation in St. Petersburg, Florida at a resort for a week and paid our way. They lived in Pittsburg so we met them there. It was a fun time being all together and they loved having the time with baby Abby, and also Matt, they were very good to him.

We all took turns watching Abby around the pool, as she had no problem running right off the edge into the water and sinking! Boy, she was fast! This episode would happen time after time. We would pull her out and she would be smiling and laughing, ready to do it again. She is still a "water bug" to this day and will dive into the ocean at 57 degrees! Matthew also was loving the pool, the beach, the warm water, but the sun was not his friend. The exposure was intense, and even with sunscreen he fried and ended up sick with sun poisoning. He was in agony. We treated it and he slept through an entire afternoon. After that he stayed under the cabana, covered in Aloe Vera gel, and not very happy about it at all.

Our wonderful trip ended and we were back to our life in San Diego: John working his gardening job for the city schools with me working three days a week at the bank so I could be home with Abby. We had a woman from our church come in the other two days a week to stay with Abby. She was the director of the drama team we had joined at the church. She was actually a nurse in the movie *M.A.S.H.* and she was a hoot! Once while watching Abby, she locked her in the car strapped into her car seat. Of course, Abby had no idea and sat there smiling as Dawn banged on the windows and yelled for help. A person nearby was able to unlock the car quickly and all was well.

Money was tight, but we managed. My dad would often ask if I needed any help, but I didn't say yes very often. He and mom would often take us out to dinner or have us over. My oldest brother and his wife also had us over a lot. We spent just about every weekend doing activities with their family and then would pool our food resources together and have a potluck at their house.

We continued the tradition of playing football out in their cul-de-sac, now with our own kids joining in. His wife became like a sister to me; always willing to watch the kids and include us in family outings; we had such fun together and built lasting memories. But there was heartbreak on the horizon.

Their oldest son, my nephew, was getting into trouble here in San Diego. He began to get involved with a bad group of kids who led him to drugs and down a road that would certainly end in destruction.

Their family made a big, but necessary decision: to leave San Diego and move to a small town outside of Salem, Oregon. It was a good choice, but we missed them terribly. Weekends were never the same.

The praise report: my nephew gave his life to Christ, married, and plays drums in his church band; he coaches soccer, runs his own business, and has four amazing sons who all love the Lord!

Riding the Fence Really Hurts!

This progress was a process, with many hurdles to overcome, but we learned that God remains faithful when we surrender completely to His will for our lives, jump off the fence, and keep our focus on Him!

> God remains faithful when we surrender completely to His will for our lives, jump off the fence, and keep our focus on Him!

Chapter 9
IN AND OUT OF THE CAGE

Abby was almost two years old, and I knew with our financial situation, it was time to go back to work full time. I found a wonderful woman around the corner from us who had a daycare in her home ... sweet Lillian. Abby thrived there, and it was nice having her so close to home.

John would pick her up when he got off work around 3:30pm and bring her home to watch *The Three Stooges* with him. Our yard still had rocks and no grass had ever been planted. I continued to be the cheerleader giving lots of suggestions and trying to motivate, but all to no avail.

He was a good husband and loved me deeply; he always paid the bills he was responsible for, and helped around the house, and he kept things neat and tidy. But was that enough? I pondered, "What to do, what to do?" The frustration was increasing and my patience was running thin while my resentment grew. Why didn't he want to improve our lives and take care of us? Why was he okay with struggling to get by? Why was our livelihood always left up to me? God, help us!

My dad and I talked about John starting his own landscaping business. My dad would provide the startup costs and we would pay him back as the business grew. When I shared the idea with John, it seemed he was getting on board and excited about this new adventure. I sure was!

Then, as in the past, "Negative Ned" showed up, and all the "what ifs" and "I don't knows" and "It's too much to take on …" returned. I knew that this "monkey" was out of the cage again and screaming his lies, doubts, and fears into John's ear. John decided there was no way he could start a business and take on the stress. He was happy doing his gardening jobs for the schools, being on his own, and taking the monkey in and out of the cage anytime he felt he needed to escape. It broke my heart, because I knew, he knew, we both knew that he was letting me down (and God), and his self-worth was suffering. He would apologize, ask for forgiveness, and try to explain to me that he just couldn't take on anything that stressed him out.

If I had known then what I know now, through my many years of counseling those who suffer from addiction and depression, we would have gotten him into the AA program and on an antidepressant to help with anxiety. Regardless, I would continue praying for patience, strength, and healing for John. However, my strength was waning.

I would think often about being married to someone whom I could lean upon, who would be my pillar of strength, who had ambition and the will to be the best he could be. "What would that be like?" I wondered.

Working in the bank, opening accounts and taking loan applications, I was in touch daily with successful men and women, those starting businesses, moving into new homes, buying nice cars, sending their kids to private schools, in touch with dreams and goals. I envied them and felt stuck. Of course, there were always *very* successful men who would flirt and flatter, and suggest, "Let me take you away from all of this." I would laugh and remind them I was a married woman. But I would daydream about what it would be like to be taken care of and not be worried about money, having someone who would be a pillar of strength for me.

It seemed, on reflection, that in both my marriages it was me who was leaned on for strength and to get things done. However, I repressed the thoughts and stayed committed to my marriage and family. I hoped, "Things would certainly get better ..." and I would continue to strive to make our lives improve.

We had been married eight years, and the vacation when Abby was a baby had been our last. Abby was now three and Matthew eleven, almost twelve. I had opened a savings account and was putting money aside for a family vacation. The kids were excited about a trip to somewhere fun. According to my accounting, we would have $1,500.00 in savings when the next statement arrived. When the mail came, I excitedly opened the bank statement to review my progress. My heart dropped and my anger rose as I looked at almost a zero balance in the vacation savings account. I questioned, "Where had the money gone?" Oh no, don't tell me!

I took a deep breath and tried to control my temper when John and I talked about the savings account. I wanted a reasonable explanation for the withdrawal of our vacation funds which had been so carefully deposited each time I got paid, in anticipation of our much-needed vacation. His explanation, "I had to use it; I needed it, I needed it."

Again, the monkey was out of the cage and now out of control. I felt defeated, hopeless and helpless, knowing I couldn't fix this.

Even with all the prayers for healing and restoration, nothing had changed. This roller coaster continued, happy one day, depressed and using the next. My resentment grew. I questioned, "Was this it?" "Was this my future, my life?" Even my faith felt weak and the enemy was circling. I am reminded of this passage of scripture.

I Peter 5: 8 and 9 (NIV)

[8] Be alert and of sober mind. Your enemy the devil prowls around like a roaring lion looking for someone to devour. [9] Resist him, standing

firm in the faith, because you know that the family of believers throughout the world is undergoing the same kind of sufferings.

To make matters worse, Matthew was starting to act out at school and getting into fights. He was in the 6th grade getting ready to graduate and move into Junior High school. I got a call from his teacher, Mr. Goulet. He was a big, strong Frenchman who demanded respect and obedience in his classroom, but he was fair, a good teacher, and kind to the kids. I remember my son telling me if the boys weren't listening and acting up, he would pick them up by the nap of their neck and carry them outside the classroom to sit. They actually thought that was pretty cool.

Of course, that was 36 years ago; today he would be sued and fired. Mr. Goulet was worried about Matt and asked if I could come in to talk about him. His question was very direct and eye opening: "Is something going on at home? Matt seems very frustrated and wants to punch it out with anyone that will take him on. He even jumps in when a kid is getting beat up and finishes the fight taking down the kid that was winning. He's a good kid, and I'm not sure what's going on, but if this behavior continues into Junior High, he's going to get hurt by much bigger kids."

I told Mr. Goulet that there had been tension at home with his stepdad along with years of pent-up frustration, and the situation had finally reached the boiling point. I thanked the teacher for his concern for Matt, for calling me, and I told him that I would take care of it. Mama bear was about to attack! This was the straw that broke this camel's back!

Chapter 10
OKAY, SATAN, LET'S DANCE!

I wanted to take Matthew and Abby and just run away. The grass was looking greener on the other side. That familiar feeling from ten years ago was bubbling up again. Perhaps there was a "Prince Charming" wanting to whisk me away to all sorts of exciting adventures and take care of me and my children.

For example, there was that handsome, wealthy businessman who always stopped to chat with me when he came into the bank. He was constantly offering exotic trips and the promise of the "good life." He was single and seemed very eager to get to know me; or, I wondered, "Was I just another challenge to him, another notch on his belt?" I decided I would have to approach this friendship with caution and try to discern his motives. Or, another example: that other tall, handsome, shy, successful guy who would make it a point to come into the bank to sit and talk; he seemed very sweet and nice and had adorable dimples. I pondered, "Maybe I should accept his offer to go to lunch sometime."

I felt the pull of the world, the good life, excitement, travel, money, and freedom. Another scripture filled my mind. This one was Matthew 6:24 (NIV)

> "No one can serve two masters. Either you will hate the one and love the other. Or you will be devoted to the one and despise the other. You cannot love God and money."

After my meeting with Matt's teacher and seriously talking with John at length, laying out the last nine years of our lives together, I told him I felt he should move out for a trial separation. Matt's livelihood and happiness were now of utmost importance to me; my son's anger and resentment was growing stronger everyday as he pushed me away and avoided being at home as much as he could. My loving, sweet boy was angry with me and felt neglected and alone. I had to fix this!

The trial separation began. The reality of John moving out and in with a friend brought lots of tears, regrets, and heartache. Was this really happening again, another failed marriage? I also hadn't factored in how this would affect three-and-a-half-year-old Abby. I had just sent her daddy away. She would cry for him and say, "I want my daddy." It broke my heart.

John was a good, loving father to her, and he was the father Matt longed for. He would come every Wednesday to pick Abby up at pre-school and would take her on weekends. But she would still cry when I would come to get her and she had to leave him.

Matthew still had a lot of anger pent up inside that needed to be dealt with. He was coming into adolescence and his anger just exploded one evening at the house. He walked into the living room, told me he hated his life, and had a steak knife in his hand with tears running down his face. I sprung to my feet and started towards him. He backed up, and told me to back off. My heart was pounding as I pleaded with him to put the knife down, that I understood his anger and frustration. I told him that is the reason I had asked John to move out, hoping that things would be better now. I told Matt I loved him so very much, that his grandparents loved him, and that most of all God loved him. Praying, "God help him, God help me!" He finally dropped the knife and I ran to him wrapping my arms around him, both of us weeping uncontrollably. We held each other for a long time and talked.

I checked with the insurance I had through my job at the bank, and found free group counseling sessions which Matt and I could attend. He would go in with the kids' group for their sessions, and I would stay with the mothers for ours. These six sessions changed his life. He was stunned and horrified at the lives these kids (all boys) were having to endure. Beat-up by step fathers, not enough food or clothes, parents getting high, living in cars, etc. My sweet, loving boy was back, full of empathy. He was appreciating all he had and looking forward to a carefree teenage life. However, more challenges were coming … serious challenges.

John eventually moved into his own duplex and he and I knew this would be permanent. I had already started dating the "wealthy businessman" who had been pursuing me and found myself back on that God-awful fence again!

I didn't want to file for divorce, knowing John was in pain and alone. I also lay in bed many a night crying over the breakup and "the way we were" before it all fell apart. I prayed for his recovery, and I prayed for my own soul, asking for God's forgiveness as I chose to give the world a spin.

John and I together had been a strong and united front when it came to Abby, never arguing or treating each other unkindly. He told my mom once, when she was relating to him, how sad it had made her that we had split up, that he was "just grateful for the best nine years of his life he had enjoyed with me, and that those years were the happiest he had ever known."

Soon, he was also dating, but continued to pick Abby up to spend time with her, even taking her back to Pittsburg for a vacation with his immediate family. She had so much fun as they fussed over her, bought her new clothes and toys, and cherished each moment with her.

Riding the Fence Really Hurts!

John and I would file for divorce a couple years later. He agreed that I would keep the house in exchange for him not having to pay child support for Abby. He never gave me a cent or paid for anything she truly needed. She knew this, and as she got older, she didn't spend as much time with him, and felt she couldn't depend on him. This condition would come to haunt her in her future relationships with men.

My "spin" with the world was in full swing. I no longer went to church, nor did my children. We pulled away from our Christian friends. We did not desire to be judged and did not want to be honest with them. I knew I would feel guilty for my lifestyle. It just didn't feel right to try and ride the fence, with one leg in the church and one leg in the world.

Another scripture came to mind. This one was from the book of Revelation 3:15 and 16 (NIV)

> [15] I know your deeds, that you are neither cold nor hot. I wish you were either one or the other! [16] So, because you are lukewarm—neither hot nor cold—I am about to spit you out of my mouth.

For the first time, I had jumped off the fence into the world instead of back into the wise and loving hands of God. I thanked Jesus for loving me even in my backsliding and sin. I knew I still loved Him and that He would forever be my Lord and Savior. But for now, after all the years of serving

Him and striving to do the right thing, I chose to rebel in my 30s, and let the lure of the world, and what I thought it had to offer, have its way with me. The "cold" would eventually become unbearable and the shivering extremely uncomfortable.

> I had jumped off the fence into the world instead of back into the wise and loving hands of God. I thanked Jesus for loving me even in my backsliding and sin.
> I knew I still loved Him and that He would forever be my Lord and Savior.

Chapter 11
New Job, New Loves, New Life

It became evident that I would need to find a higher paying job. I was now raising two kids on my own, with one paycheck.

I told my boss that I would like to be considered for management training. I had already been taught all the positions at the branch level to be a "branch specialist," but it didn't do much for my paycheck.

I was accepted into the management training program, and the training began. It involved trips to L.A. with other trainees in the program, with overnight stays, an expense account, etc.

It was a great adventure and a wonderful training experience that I excelled at. I felt excitement about moving ahead with my career and taking care of my children and myself.

Of course, my parents were there to stay with the kids when I had to travel, and mom would always leave the fridge packed with food and the kids were provided with new shoes, or pants, or whatever she saw the need to be. I thanked God for the faithfulness and love of my parents. My dad was so proud and supportive; he was always my cheerleader, reminding me I could do anything I put my mind to. This confidence was something he instilled in my brothers and me early on.

> Confidence was something my dad instilled in my brothers and me early on.

Part of the bank's management training included being placed in various branches as an assistant to the operations manager. This included the training and overseeing of tellers, opening the vault in the morning and closing it at night. It also involved learning how to lead, motivate, and improve the overall operation of the branch. I loved it, especially the teaching and motivating of others, and improving operational procedures which needed a fresh eye. I was seeing qualities in myself that I didn't even know I had. I noticed quickly that encouraging others to do their best and pursue their dreams were investments they loved to receive and put into practice.

One of the branches in which I was placed, was in a bad area of town. This branch had been robbed several times. There were actual bullet holes in the wall!

Riding the Fence Really Hurts!

The assistant manager I would be working with was a "Debbie Downer ..." a person very unhappy with her job and life in general. The staff was afraid of her and walked on egg shells to keep her from going off on them. They soon embraced my encouragement and upbeat attitude, and I became a counselor and friend, but I was always respected as their boss.

A few of the gals on the teller line were single and would invite me to go out dancing with them. I finally accepted their offer and had a ball dancing and drinking 7up. We would do this several times. They also invited me to be a model in a show their friend had put together ... this was fun, too. That old feeling of being centerstage, that I loved, flooded back. The world was looking pretty good and I was having fun ... but for how long?

My training at the various branches ended, and I was recommended for a job at the downtown branch in San Diego in the loan division upstairs. I was out of the operations of branch banking and began assisting the loan officers with their commercial high-end clients in bringing their demand accounts to our bank along with their loans.

It was nice being out of hectic branch management and learning this side of banking. However, even with this new assignment and responsibilities, my income was nowhere near what it needed to be for the kids and me to get by. My credit card debt would soar at Christmas time when I had to buy everything on credit and then slowly pay it back with the minimum payment each month.

The relationship with the wealthy businessman ran its course. His plans to take me on cruises and trips never happened. I wanted to go, but my devotion to my children had to come first and I couldn't leave them and run around the world with him. He wanted to marry, buy a new house, and start a new life together. I had just gotten out of my "other" life and I certainly didn't want to jump out of the frying pan into the fire and make yet another poor decision. Besides, other opportunities to date and be pickier this time around were popping up at every turn. I figured, "Might as well keep my options open."

My sister-in-law invited me out to play soccer. I had watched Matthew play but really didn't know all the rules or positions. We had never played soccer in high school. I was introduced to the team and given a jersey to put on as I sat on the sidelines watching, never imagining I would be put into the game. All of a sudden, coach told me to go into the game as a defender. His advice: "Just don't let anyone get by you and score; our goalie isn't very good." I ran in with my new jersey and borrowed cleats. I said to myself, "I can do this!" Heck, I had played football with my brothers for years and excelled on the powder puff football team in high school.

I thought I was going to pass out from running all over the field after that ball. My heart was pounding out of my chest

Riding the Fence Really Hurts!

as I stood, catching my breath in front of the goal box for a rest. The coach continued to scream, "Don't let her get by you!" He no sooner had said that when a ball was launched in my direction, headed for the goal box and a sure goal. My instincts told me the only thing to do was catch it, and I did, right inside the goal box! Whistles blew, everyone was scrambling and yelling, and the coach called me over to the sidelines. He explained that the only one who can touch the ball with their hands, was the goalie. Who knew? I certainly didn't. I was just doing what I was told ... "don't let them score!" He did congratulate me on an awesome catch, told me to take off my new jersey and put on the goalie jersey.

I would now face my first penalty kick. Someone would actually stand right in front of the goal box and kick it right at me and I was supposed to try and stop it. Also, I had to stand still and not move until the ball was kicked! I asked myself, "Okay, who came up with these crazy rules and why didn't they like goalies?" After a couple of tries (I kept moving), the ball was kicked at me hard, and low and behold, I caught it! Everyone cheered and the coach told me to stay in as goalie and informed me that was now my position. I played goalie for three years fearlessly and with many jammed fingers and kicked ribs. I eventually talked a new coach and a new team into letting me play half the game as a goalie and half on the field. This was much easier on the body.

My dating life continued and soon I was dating a referee I had met on the soccer field. Our games were in the evening after work. I would pick up Matthew, Abby would go with her dad or my folks, and we would head to the soccer fields in Ocean Beach, Rob Field. A few of the women on the team knew the referee, and they all drooled at his good looks and thought he was an excellent ref. He was, I thought, until a ball came like a bullet towards my face and I put my hands up to stop it from hitting my face. Another "no, no." "Hand ball" was called and a penalty kick was called for. I pleaded my case with the ref, telling him I was trying to protect my face, and my nose was bleeding as I spoke. He told me he understood and that he, too, would want to protect such a pretty face, but it was still a penalty. I was not a happy camper and stormed to the sidelines.

He followed Matt and me out of the parking lot in his car, and when we stopped at the light, he jumped out and came to my window. He asked if I was still mad at him and could he make it up to me. He wanted my number; I didn't give it to him. He asked me where I worked and I told him for Security Pacific Bank. He said that he, too, was in the finance business. The light turned and we were off. He called all the branches and finally tracked me down. Flowers, candy, Mrs. Fields Cookies, and poems were flooding the office.

We went out to lunch, and "Mr. Rico Suave" (a made-up name denoting smoothness and superficial graciousness) had his hooks in me. He was so charming, he loved to dance, and he was devoted to his three sons; he was part of a big family (one of twelve kids), and a semi-pro tennis player. He would teach me how to play, being very patient; he had taught tennis to many kids and adults. Little did I know at that time that he had his hooks in many other women, including the mothers of the kids he was teaching and another gal I played soccer with!

It didn't take long for my suspicions to come to light. I was turning into a jealous, insecure, angry, nervous, and very sad person. But I stayed and listened to his lies and excuses of why he didn't show up when plans were made. He had an explanation for everything. Everyone and everything took precedence over me and my kids. I felt like I was going crazy.

I decided I would do the same things and start seeing other guys behind his back: a dentist, and a VP from the bank, all the while feeling guilty and broken inside. God and I would have conversations about this new life I was living and He would remind me of the peace and love I felt when I was asking Him to lead my life. I missed that, but Satan would remind me that I was in too deep now, living the fun and exciting life the world had to offer. He would prod me, "No turning back, and you know you're just going to keep sinning," continually making me feel no longer acceptable to God.

The relationship with "Mr. Rico Suave" would take a sad turn when his athletic oldest son, a senior in high school who was being scouted to play basketball at college, was thrown from his three-wheeler dirt bike, broke his neck and became a quadriplegic at age seventeen. It was a parent's worst nightmare aside from losing a child.

Weekends were spent visiting the son at a rehab facility for patients who were paralyzed; an entire wing was devoted to children aged seventeen and younger. Abby and I would go see him at times, and Abby would chatter and laugh with the young children, wondering why they couldn't get up and play with her.

They loved when she came and would light up when they saw her. We would pray for them all.

I felt like a whining, neglected child as we fell lower on "Rico Suave's" totem pole. As expected, less and less time would be given to our toxic relationship. He needed to be with his family.

It was time to move on, let go, and be honest with myself. God's voice softly reminded me that He was a good Father and was protecting me, trying to gather me back up into His arms.

These were the questions I asked myself: "When would I trust Him again with my life? How many more frogs did I have to kiss? Why couldn't I trust Him to bring me the one He had chosen?"

Riding the Fence Really Hurts!

> It was time to move on, let go, and be honest with myself. God's voice softly reminded me that He was a good Father and was protecting me, trying to gather me back up into His arms.

I thanked God for my Bible upbringing and for learning scripture. I remembered Jesus saying in John 10:10 (NKJV) New King James Version®. Copyright © 1982 by Thomas Nelson. Used by permission. All rights reserved.

> "The thief does not come except to steal, and to kill, and to destroy. I have come that you may have life, and that you may have it more abundantly."

Matt was in high school now, dating, playing sports, and popular. Abby was attending the School of Creative and Performing Arts with kids from 5th to 12th grade, exposed to all kinds of different lifestyles.

I wondered, "What kind of example had I become for my precious children?"

Chapter 12
Cowboys, Rodeos, and Radio

I had never been to a rodeo in my life. I grew up just ten minutes from the beach and had never traveled that far east into San Diego County.

Just before I was to start my new banking job in the commercial loan division, I was asked to fill in temporarily as the Operations Manager at our Lakeside branch. I was happy to help, but where was Lakeside? It was going to be about a 30-minute drive from my house I was told, out in the country, "… you know, where they have the rodeos." No, I didn't know and I wasn't familiar with the rodeo scene, cowboy boots, country music, or big belt buckles. Well, that was all about to change, along with my idea of country folk, southern drawls, and dusty cowboys.

It felt like I had been put on a movie set in Dodge City with Mr. Dillon and Kitty on *Gunsmoke*, and I was playing the part of the stuck-up city girl.

Judy Bowen

The first thing I saw when entering Lakeside was the big rodeo area. The town was very homey with a real country feel and loads of mom-and-pop businesses. I arrived at the Lakeside branch of the bank and received a warm welcome from the staff who showed me around the office, gave me keys, explained the various places to eat around town, and then we opened the doors for business.

Right away I could see a difference in these customers compared to the "city folk" I was accustomed to doing business with. They were smiling and friendly and asking if I was new and where I was from. They were patient, too, and saying, "No problem darlin', take your time." It was a breath of fresh air and made for a peaceful working experience. It also brought back memories of the kind folks in Texas and the familiar "ya'll." I got right back into that expression, so fun and easy to say.

It was getting close to closing time on a Friday night when a cowboy in a starched white shirt, tight wrangler jeans, cowboy boots, a big hat, and bigger belt buckle walked up to my teller window. He gave me a big ole smile and said, "Well hi, darlin', you're new here. I'm fixin' to go to Vegas for the National Rodeo competition and I need me some cash." I smiled and asked him for his account number, hopped off my stool to check his signature in the signature card file (as he watched my every move closely), and came back with six crisp $100 dollar bills. I told him to have a good time and that it sounded like a fun trip. His response was, "Do you want to come with me?" and he laughed. I laughed, too, and told him. "No, thank you." He placed his bills in his pocket, tipped his hat, gave me a big ole smile, and off he went.

He continued to come into the bank for his banking needs and gather more information on me and my status. He was easy to talk to and very polite. I was also running into him when I would go out to pick up something for lunch, or to get a coffee, or run into a store. He seemed to be everywhere where I was. This couldn't be a coincidence.

It was Valentine's Day and I was still seeing "Rico Suave'" off and on. I didn't expect much from him on V Day since he was dealing with his paralyzed son and his other two boys and their sadness. So, when the Cowboy asked me what my big plans were for V Day with my boyfriend, I told him nothing was planned. He said, "That's just sad, that ain't right." When I left work that night there was a dozen red roses on the hood of my car with a sweet note telling me a beautiful woman like me deserved roses on Valentine's Day. Very sweet.

Of course, he was in the bank the next day and I thanked him for the roses. He asked me to lunch, then to dinner, then to the movies, and we started to see each other often. He knew I was still involved with "Mr. Suave," but knew I wasn't being treated well and that the relationship was failing. He was persistent, generous, and kind, and was soon asking me to invite my kids to join us for burgers and out to the movies. Matt wasn't impressed and called him a red-neck.

He and his dad had their own trucking business and owned the rights to hauling all the new Toyota's in from Long Beach to San Diego. They also raised cattle. He also had a small ranch with horses, and was a two-time World Champion Team Roper. He had to explain to me what that was. Abby loved the horses, and he would walk her around the coral, her sitting up on his rodeo horse, Blondie, for as long as she wanted. He was crazy about her.

We were soon going to rodeos and watching him and his partner rope, along with all the other rodeo events. Before the rodeo would start, he would put Abby up with him on his horse and walk or trot around the arena. She would beam with delight.

We were getting to know the town folk by name and we were adored by this guy. Anytime I would mention that I needed something it would be bought and delivered to my house the next day. I would feel guilty about all of this, knowing I was still seeing "Mr. Suave" off and on. Although, I did tell "Suave" about my Cowboy and all the attention we were receiving. He laughed and jabbed, "You with a cowboy? Right … that's ridiculous." But I knew he was off doing whatever he felt like with whoever was willing, and I felt no shame in letting him know that I wasn't sitting around waiting for his attention anymore. It was time to move on.

Riding the Fence Really Hurts!

My family thought the Cowboy was a wonderful, giving, caring man and didn't know what else I could possibly need in a man. But I felt like I was living two different lives. One in "my" world (beach, tennis, dancing, proper grammar, shorts, sandals, business clothes, and banking) and his world with rodeos, horses, cattle, country music, poor grammar, boots and chaps. He didn't seem to fit into "my" world with my friends, and I was a little embarrassed to bring him around them and shamed for feeling that way. He was a wonderful man wanting to take care of us, but once again, here I was on the fence wanting, needing to make the right decisions, this time for me *and* my children. Something was not sitting right in my heart.

My time working in commercial lending was good, but I still was barely getting by financially. I went to my boss, a great guy who was so happy with my work, and asked him what I could do to move up and make good money. He told me I needed to become an AVP (Assistant Vice President) and that would mean going back to college and taking an accounting class. All the college level management courses I had taken didn't include accounting. I agreed to go to the local community college and enrolled into the class. Of course, this meant working all day, coming home briefly to make dinner for the kids, then rushing to my class and relying on my parents to babysit.

While my confusion on whether to stay with the cowboy loomed over my head, so did this class that I hated. *So* boring!

And it was taking me away at night from my kids. Surely there was another way to make more money, something I was better suited for.

I asked God to help me and show me the way. My need for Him and His wisdom weighed heavily on me, reminding me He had always had the best plan for my life, and my plan, the world's plan, certainly wasn't filled with the joy and peace I had when I was following Him. Even though I had pulled away from Him for three years, I remembered yet another beautiful verse and promise:

Romans 8:38-39 (NIV)

"For I am convinced that neither death, nor life, neither angels nor demons, neither the present nor the future, nor any powers, neither height nor depth, nor anything else in all creation, will be able to separate us from the love of God that is Christ Jesus our Lord."

I was still and would always be His beloved daughter, and He longed for me to come to Him for comfort, guidance, and direction.

Riding the Fence Really Hurts!

> I was still and would always be His beloved daughter, and He longed for me to come to Him for comfort, guidance, and direction.

I had only been to a few accounting classes when my mom called to tell me she had randomly run into my dad's former secretary (they were both retired now) and was catching up with her on the family news. Her daughter, Diane, was about my age and had a good job with the government. Our families would boat together and entertain in each other's homes when she was employed as my dad's secretary for many years.

When my mom asked about Diane, she was told that Diane had left the government job and was now working in the radio business, selling radio ads for a local station we all knew, KCBQ, one of the original rock stations in San Diego. She told my mom that Diane was the top seller in San Diego and making crazy good money and having so much fun. My mom then told her about my situation, being divorced, two kids, trying to make ends meet. My mom asked if it would be okay for me to call Diane and chat. She got the number and passed it on to me after telling me of Diane's success story. I couldn't dial the phone fast enough!

Diane and I met, a divine appointment; she was a believer and had multitudinous wisdom to pass onto me both professionally and spiritually as together she and I reviewed my past three and a half years. She thought I would do well in radio sales and told me she would tell her sales manager about me and have her call me to set up a meeting.

I had a two-hour lunch with her very outgoing sales manager, and she told me she thought I would excel in the radio industry as well. Sadly, she didn't have any openings in sales but gave me a list of sales managers at other stations, told me to call them and tell them she recommended me and start interviewing. I thanked God for answered prayer, and opening this door. I dropped the accounting class, and was on a mission to get hired into the exciting and fun world of radio.

I knew that the country western station, KSON, was very popular and a top-rated station in San Diego. I called there first for an interview with the sales manager. He had me come in and was very gracious with the time he spent with me, but had no current sales positions open. I would schedule these interviews during my one-hour lunch break from my banking job downtown and rush back to the office. I was encouraged by my first interview and excited for the next which would be with another top-rated rock and roll station KGB 101.5, owned at that time by Brown Broadcasting, which also owned an AM "oldies" station, KPOP, my mom's favorite. I kept thinking, "I have nothing to lose; I have a job and I will continue these interviews until something comes up," feeling confident inside that I was following God's lead, and that old familiar peace came over me.

Riding the Fence Really Hurts!

I was still on the fence, but this time I had one foot firmly placed on God's side, with the other still dangling in the world. However, I could feel my faith and trust in Him returning and my need for the world fading. I chose to continue to ask Him for direction, confident He would grant wisdom and understanding, and make His ways known.

The interview at KGB/KPOP was a hoot. The sales manager was very open and friendly and seemed like someone I would really enjoy working with. I told him how I knew Diane and he, too, knew her and her reputation of being a go-getter, top seller, and told me he had interviewed her back when she was trying to get into the radio biz and blew it by, not hiring her.

She, like me, had had no experience in the business and would need to be trained. This was my story exactly. I told him of my experience in banking, selling bank products to commercial clients, going on calls with the commercial loan reps, and my success in bringing those clients over to our banking system from our competitors. He told me he was just starting the interview process which would be a couple of weeks, and was looking for someone with experience in the industry, but he would follow up with me when he and the manager decided which way to go. I smiled, thanked him for his time, and walked to his office door to leave.

With my hand on the doorknob, I turned and said to him, "I hope you're not making another mistake that you're going to regret by not hiring me, like you did with Diane." He threw his head back in laughter and said, "Okay, I'll keep that in mind."

I rushed back to my office and no sooner got in my chair when my phone rang. It was the sales manager from KGB with whom I had just met, and he asked if I could come back the next day for another interview, this time with him and the General Manager.

I was so excited I could hardly work and called my mom and dad to tell them the news. They promised to be praying for me as they always did.

I left early for lunch the next day wanting to have plenty of time for my meeting at the radio station with the sales manager and the GM. I was brought back to the sales manager's office once again, and sat down. He told me that he could hardly believe what I said as I was leaving his office the day before, and that he had told the GM about it and he, too, wanted to meet me. We immediately went to his nice office with a private bathroom and shower (that impressed me), and he said I had made quite an impression on the sales manager, especially with the comment I made about Diane when I was leaving, and that he wanted to meet me, to see if I was worthy of the time it takes to train someone with no experience.

Riding the Fence Really Hurts!

He was very direct and professional. I, too, wanted to be professional, honest, and direct. I told them both I was a single mom of two children and understood that this would be a commissioned sales position, but I had to bring home at least $1,500 a month to get by. This meant they would have to assign me a couple of accounts right away on which I could make commission. Of course, we talked about my experience and training at the bank over the past fifteen years, that I wasn't completely green or just coming out of college. They thanked me for coming in, said they would discuss everything, and get back to me. I asked when I should be expecting their call. More smiles and "soon" was the response. My take was that they appreciated my confidence and honesty and could see I had no problem holding my own while showing respect.

I would get another call that afternoon offering me the job! I could hardly wait to rush into the VP's office and turn in my resignation. He had been very good to me, a good boss and mentor, and he now questioned my move into a commissioned position explaining its ups and downs and told me, "I hope you're not back here a year from now asking me for your job back."

I stood tall and told him I knew this was an enormous opportunity for me and my kids and I would never look back. I would make it work! Let's rock 'n' roll, baby!

Chapter 13
THE BALANCING ACT—
DIAMONDS AND A MUSTANG

I pulled up and parked in the KGB parking lot. I was told that all employees enter around the back and are buzzed in until they have a key. I sat in my car and gave myself the "talk" I always gave myself when starting a new job: "You've got this. In six months, you'll have it all down and will be doing great. You're going to thrive at this job and God is going to give you the wisdom you need to grasp it all." I prayed, "Thank you, God, for opening this door and giving me a new start."

I was buzzed in and walked down a long hallway lined with studios. The morning show, "Burger and Prescott," the names of two popular radio hosts in San Diego, was "live" on the air. I had to stop and watch them in action. I had listened to them so many times on the radio and always wondered what they looked like. They didn't have a "face for radio," but were good-looking guys. I gave a little wave and they smiled and waved back. This was already exciting and I hadn't even been shown my desk yet.

The sales manager's office was at the end of the hall and he motioned for me to come in. He also asked a seasoned radio sales rep (we called ourselves Account Executives) Lisa, to come in to meet me and get me all organized. I was told she was the organizing queen, and she didn't disappoint. She made it all seem easy and she would become my mentor and very dear friend. However, when we were called into the conference room for the sales meeting, I looked around the room for a seat, smiled at all the new faces and sat down. They all smirked at each other when Lisa walked in and told me "You're in my seat." I jumped up embarrassed and said, "Sorry! I didn't know there was assigned seating." They all laughed and the tension was broken. But I made sure not to sit in that seat again! All other seats were up for grabs.

I soon found that there was a lot of freedom in outside sales, and it took focused discipline to make calls, accept "no's", make more calls, and go on sales calls. It was much easier to go on calls at a mall and do a little shopping, or take long lunches with colleagues or friends. I was even enjoying afternoon sports games Matt would play in at 3:00 p.m.: soccer, football, track, and volleyball. I always made it back to the office to finish the day but with a sense of guilt at times, knowing I needed to work harder to get new clients. I needed to find the right balance.

I was enjoying the face-to-face sales calls but was finding it difficult to close the sale. I knew I needed to ask my sales manager for help and finally did after many months on the job and only a few sales. He was happy to go on my next call with me and on as many calls as was needed, since I needed to assess what I was doing wrong.

I had a very good client lined up for us to see; he was already on other radio stations and was perfect for KGB which targeted a male dominated listening audience. He was a brake specialist. We arrived and went back into his office. We chatted about all kinds of things and I talked and talked about how great our station was and showed him graphs and charts to back up my words. My sales manager didn't say much but let me carry the ball and run with it. We were there almost an hour. At the close, we shook hands and he told me he would think about it. There were big smiles all around, and the sales manager and I were out the door.

The ride back to the office was an eye opener. My boss told me I was all over the place, talked too much, didn't ask enough questions, and the biggest issue: I didn't schedule a follow-up appointment before we left. The very thing you *always* do when ending a meeting is schedule a follow-up meeting. It became obvious why I wasn't closing deals. We would get back to the office, sit in my sales manager's office, and put together a script that I would learn and use on every call.

This worked for me after years of learning lines in plays. I kept a cheat sheet with me on upcoming calls until I was confident in my lines and no longer needed it. I then began asking important questions, a part of a CNA (Customer Needs Analysis) to determine if the client was a good fit for our station, to determine if they had the budget, what kind of commercial they had thought about airing, etc. It was the turning point in my sales numbers, and eliminated the frustration that had been plaguing me.

After my first full year in sales, I had almost doubled my income from what I had made at the bank. Yep, I would never look back.

Part of the excitement working in radio were the perks! For example: movie and concert tickets, sporting events tickets, lift tickets, expense accounts, and "trade" with restaurants around town. We would exchange (trade) radio advertising for "funny money" used to eat at their establishments, kind of like monopoly money. We enjoyed free, delicious meals. We would use these restaurants to entertain clients. There were even amazing trips for which I would qualify, and I would go on these trips with clients who spent a big chunk of their advertising budget with us in their first quarter.

Promotions were also big deals for clients, and these promotions would give them added value to their advertising package. Tents popped up in their car lots, a prize wheel was used, and food was available from another client who desired on-air mentions. All this added to the extra announcements

Riding the Fence Really Hurts!

they would receive, as the radio hosts throughout the day would talk about an upcoming event.

As a newer sales rep, I was given some nightclubs to call on and more promotional events. This meant taking an on-air celebrity out at night to the club, giving away prizes and watching people get drunk and pushy with the very cute and sexy radio personality. This would most always end with some guy thinking our celebrity was in love with him and he would start stalking her at the stations. A guard would have to be hired to protect her and walk her to her car, and the police would get involved as well. I was *so* relieved when a newer rep was hired and I could hand off the club promotions.

As mentioned, my mom loved our AM station KPOP; they played the oldies like Sinatra, Tony Bennet, Patsy Cline, Elvis, and more. She would tell me to call on all her favorite places to shop so they would advertise, and told everyone she knew that I worked for KPOP. I excelled in selling KPOP and enjoyed setting up "live" on-air remotes at places like the Hotel Del Coronado or Seaport Village. The faithful audience would all come out to see their favorite on-air host, Jerry Bishop, do his show "live" and were thrilled to be there. My mom was always in attendance. I would soon become the top seller for KPOP.

My relationships with "Rico Suave" and Cowboy were off again, then on again. More and more I was feeling the pull of

God to come back to Him and do things His way. He was blessing me and I was so grateful, and I thanked Him often for His faithfulness to me and my children.

Again, I was reminded of a verse, quoting Jesus from the book of the Gospel of John, John 10:28-29 (NIV):

> [28] "I give them eternal life, and they shall never perish; no one will snatch them out of my hand. [29] My Father, who has given them to me, is greater than all; no one can snatch them out of my Father's hand."

Once we belong to Him, He never lets go. We may stray from Him but He is always holding onto us, and asking us to return.

Once we belong to Him, He never lets go. We may stray from Him but He is always holding onto us, and asking us to return.

I was able to save money, refinance the house, and get enough out to pay off my credit card debt and get rid of the ugly gray rocks and replace them with grass! I also expanded the little patio in the backyard and had Matt and Abby put their names in the wet cement with the date. The imprints are still there. I know this because Matt and his family are living in that house, and now his children, our grandchildren, have

Riding the Fence Really Hurts!

their names in an extended cement patio. Imprints remain, unlike "fence relationships!"

I knew in my heart that neither "Suave"' or Cowboy were right for me. Both had asked to marry me.

I had to get off this fence and make some serious decisions! I was so confused and asked my crazy, wild, girlfriend if she had any suggestions. She actually did have some, and referred me to her therapist who was also a Christian. I called and made an appointment, and told her of my dilemma with these two guys, both totally opposite and each having some of what I was looking for, but neither having all I felt I needed in a man. She asked if I could change either one of them to be exactly what I needed and my answer was, "No." She continued with this counsel: "It would seem there will be someone else God has planned for you who will come along in His timing." It made perfect sense; I left and never went back again.

On a side note, that wild, crazy, alcoholic girlfriend came to know Jesus as her Savior after she and I talked many times about Jesus and her need for Him. She married, has two grown, beautiful daughters, and a wonderful husband. We are still the best of friends and when they come to visit, we talk non-stop about Jesus. She has also been an AA sponsor to many over the years and loves pouring into the lives of those in need. Even during my confusion and rebellion God used my story to bring her to Him!

> Even during my confusion and rebellion God used my story to bring her to Him!

I totally called things off with "Suave" and continued to try and make things work with Cowboy. He bought new clothes to please me and to fit in better with my friends. He lost weight, I taught him to play tennis, and took him to some radio events; all the while feeling guilty that I felt I needed to change him if he wanted to be with me. How selfish and self-centered could I be?

He continued to shower me with unexpected gifts of diamond earrings, bracelets, necklaces, and rings. He thought I would wear the diamond ring on my left hand, but I placed it on my right, explaining we were not engaged. I could see he was disappointed and I always offered to give these gifts back to him, knowing in my heart this was not a long-term relationship, and that I was being cruel.

Why couldn't I just accept this sweet man for who he was? I would soon find out, but not before he bought me a brand-new blue Ford Mustang that was sitting in my driveway when I got home from work.

Chapter 14
VONS GROCERY STORE, AND DIMPLES

I felt like I was operating on auto pilot: kids, work, promotion events for the stations, spending time with Cowboy (knowing he wasn't the one), and waiting on God to usher in that special someone the therapist talked about.

I decided to follow the advice of some speaker I had heard and write down all the qualities I wanted in a man and lay it before the Lord:

1. Believed in God
2. Good looking
3. Athletic
4. Good paying job
5. Owned a house
6. Owned a nice car
7. Kind, gentle
8. Ego in check
9. Someone strong on whom I could lean, and one who would take care of us and not depend on me to do it
10. And the big **Number 10**: He would love and accept my children

I prayed, "Okay, Lord, there it is. I'm willing to place this before You and trust Your timing and that You know what is best for me."

Proverbs 16:3 (NIV)

"Commit to the Lord whatever you do and He will establish your plans."

It felt right to be seeking the Lord's guidance and making my way back home to Him. He had never failed me in the past when I had laid my plans before Him, and I knew even now as I was still blowing it, that He was there wanting and willing to lead and guide me to the abundant life He had for me.

It was a Friday night with the weekend ahead of us. Cowboy stayed with Abby and I went up to the local Vons grocery store to pick up supplies. Sweatpants on, hair pulled up in a pony tail, I leaned on the basket and slowly perused the isles, almost in a trance. It had been a long week and I was tired and feeling down. It was relaxing listening to the piped in music and to be strolling around the store on my own.

As I passed the checkout area, I noticed a tall, handsome, well-dressed man in one of the lines. He looked at me and I returned his glance. Simultaneously we recognized each other. It was "Dimples …" the tall, shy, cute dimpled client who had come in weekly to sit and chat when I worked at the bank.

Riding the Fence Really Hurts!

> It felt right to be seeking the Lord's guidance and making my way back home to Him. He had never failed me in the past when I had laid my plans before Him, and I knew even now as I was still blowing it, that He was there wanting and willing to lead and guide me to the abundant life He had for me.

Before I'd left that branch, and went into the management training program, I did agree to go to lunch with him. There were no sparks; I was just getting into the single life and dating and didn't want to pursue anything or anyone. I had left the branch and I never saw him again. I often wondered about him; he was so sweet, kind, and good looking. I figured he was probably happily remarried by now. It had been over four years.

I said, "Gary?" and he responded, "Judy?" He stepped out of line so we could talk, and I asked him what he was doing in this Vons, so far away from where he lived. He told me he was having dinner with his girlfriend who lived in the apartments across from the store and was buying wine. It was his first time ever in this store. He asked me if I was still in banking, or if I had remarried, or if I had a boyfriend.

I explained my new career in radio, (KGB was his favorite station), that I had never remarried, and that I did have a boyfriend, but that this boyfriend was not the right one for me. He said, "Same for me; Can I call you?" I gave him my business card and asked him to call me at work, knowing Cowboy was at my place for the weekend.

My heart was pounding out of my chest. I pondered, "Was he always this good looking and tall, and that smile with those dimples!?" I was actually anxious for the weekend to end and to get back to work on Monday, anticipating a phone call. Could this man be the "someone else" the therapist had spoken of? Somewhere deep in my heart, I knew he was.

I told Cowboy over the weekend that I could not in any way accept his generous gift of a new Mustang car. He reminded me that I needed a more dependable car and asked if he could buy me a less expensive new car. Again, I declined the extravagant offer. I knew I wanted to pursue this possible new relationship with Gary which confirmed Cowboy was not the one for me. If Cowboy had been the right one, I concluded I wouldn't still be looking. Cowboy said he would take the Mustang back in a couple of days, and for me to drive it until then. I drove it to work on Monday.

I got right to work and tried to forget about the anticipated phone call from Gary. It was still morning when the phone rang and I picked up; it was him, asking how my weekend was, and would I like have lunch? I told him I would be out and about on calls but that I could come down to his work place in National City. He was the sales manager for a large wholesale lumber operation near the docks. I drove up in the new Mustang, then walked into his office and was introduced

Riding the Fence Really Hurts!

to his secretary and staff. When we walked out to go to lunch and he saw the new Mustang he exclaimed, "Wow!" I told him I would explain it all at lunch, and I did.

We talked for quite some time, catching up on our lives over the past four-plus years. I was surprised to find out that he had checked up on me through a woman friend who played soccer in our league. She had told him I was dating "Suave." I then told him what a nightmare that relationship had been for me and that I couldn't trust that guy as far as I could throw him. I also told Gary that Cowboy had basically rescued me from that toxic relationship, that he had been very kind and generous to me and my kids, but that we didn't have a lot in common. I explained that I knew in my heart I couldn't spend the rest of my life with him. I explained the new Mustang and that it was going back to the dealer the next day. He told me he had been casually dating and at one time had become serious about one woman with whom he had almost moved to Oregon, but decided he couldn't leave his only daughter, Breianna, who lived in San Diego and was seven years old. She was the same age as Abby!

Gary and I met for several lunches over the next week or so. We were both smitten, the attraction was strong, and it was nice that we already knew each other.

Thanksgiving was coming up and he mentioned he would be going with friends to Arizona. He mentioned that his girlfriend had been invited to go, but that he told her he would rather go alone and no longer intended to pursue that relationship. That comment made me happy and I knew that while he was gone, I would end things with Cowboy. I told Gary that I would. We both agreed that we wanted to exclusively date each other when he returned from the holiday.

I dreaded the talk I would need to have with Cowboy. It felt like another divorce of sorts, but he had done nothing wrong; in fact, just the opposite was true: he had done everything in his power to make us happy. I cried in anticipation of the sadness I knew he would be going through. I prayed that God would send him someone to love him and care for him the way he had loved and cared for me. I truly believed he deserved better. I knew he deserved to be happy, and not to be dealing with my indecision from day to day.

I told Cowboy, as I had tried to tell him before, that I needed to move on and had recently become reacquainted with someone I would like to date. I told him we were only friends at this point, but I wanted to pursue this new relationship and see where it would go. I was in tears telling him how sorry I was, and tears also streamed down his face in response.

I had the jewelry in hand that he had given me over the past two years, and was ready to return it to him, but he refused to take it back. His words to me were these: "All I ever wanted was for you to be happy, and if this guy makes you happy then I'm happy for you because you deserve all the happiness in the world." I was heaving with tears at this point, thanking him for taking such good care of us, almost wishing he had lashed out in anger and stormed off instead of being so understanding.

He gave me a big hug and kiss on the cheek, and told me he would always love me and if I ever needed him, to give him a call. He then drove off in his truck. He checked in on me frequently by phone for about a month. I explained that things were going well with Gary. Cowboy eventually stopped calling.

Even though my future was still a mystery, I felt that I had finally hopped off the fence and my feet were once again on solid ground and in God's capable hands.

My prayer:

Psalm 51:10 (KJV)

[10] Create in me a clean heart, O God; and renew a right spirit within me.

Feeling joyful and pain-free at last, I looked forward to what God had planned for me.

Judy Bowen

> Even though my future was still a mystery, I felt that I had finally hopped off the fence and my feet were once again on solid ground and in God's capable hands.

Chapter 15
GETTING TO KNOW YOU— GETTING TO KNOW ALL ABOUT YOU!

Gary returned from his trip to Arizona the weekend following Thanksgiving. He immediately called me and asked if we could get together that evening. I was home with the kids, now ages seven and fifteen, and told Matthew I had to go out for about an hour and to please watch his sister.

I was excited yet nervous to see Gary again. I questioned, "Would I still have that 'gaga' feeling I'd had before, wanting to pursue a relationship? Would he? Or had he reconsidered?"

We met up in a parking lot that overlooks Mission Bay, a gorgeous view, and talked about his trip and my sad experience with breaking it off with Cowboy. I could see that he felt empathy for Cowboy as I explained how gracious he had been, and what he said to me when we said our final goodbyes.

Gary assured me that he, too, had broken the relationship off completely from his casual girlfriend and that he was even more committed to our relationship now than before he left on his trip. I confirmed to him that I felt the same way. There were some hugs and kisses and I told him I had to get back home to the kids.

We talked on the phone many times throughout our work days and saw each other just about every day for lunch, or dinner at his place. I was impressed that he could cook! I can remember driving up to his house and seeing a lovely home in a beautiful neighborhood with lighted landscaping and a sleek black Toyota Supra in the driveway. When I walked into the house there was a full view of the bay and all the night lights twinkling outside. Everything was neat and tidy. Hallelujah!

As we continued to learn more about each other, I was happy to hear he was very athletic and had been on the track and field team in college. Plus, he skied, was an avid bike rider, and he played racquet ball almost every day. He was 6' 2" and in great shape!

I bragged a bit about my football days, dancing, acting, playing piano and, of course, my soccer experiences. Also, that I was a gym rat for a few days every week and loved the aerobic classes. I told him I had only skied a couple of times and it was brutal; he promised to teach me. This guy was checking all the right boxes but one, a very important one.

Riding the Fence Really Hurts!

I was mentally asking this question: "Did he believe in God and what was his relationship with Him?" I said a little silent prayer and jumped into that conversation with both feet.

I remember telling him of my loving upbringing and being raised in a Christian home, attending a Baptist church, and how much I loved it and loved God. He responded that his grandma had taken him to Sunday School, though his parents didn't attend, and then at age eight his parents divorced and he was told by his strict grandpa that he was now the man of the house and had to take care of his mom. His sister had moved in with their dad, not wanting to deal with a bi-polar, meanspirited, abusive mom. Gary had concluded that he simply had no choice but to stay and take it, and he did so, up until he turned eighteen and could move out, attend a local college, and be free from her abuse.

His saving grace while he was growing up in a dysfunctional home was his sweet grandma taking him to church, telling him she loved him and Jesus loved him, and his wonderful friends in the neighborhood always welcoming him into their homes. He would have a homecooked Italian dinner every Sunday night at the Giacolone house. Mrs. G. was from Sicily and the meals were authentic Italian cuisine. They were a big, loud, happy, Italian family. Gary found comfort and love in their home. He and Tony (the Giacolone's son) are still great friends to this day.

He had also been a Boy Scout for many years until he entered high school and his mom demanded that he wear his uniform to school. He refused to wear the uniform at school, knowing he would be teased. His mom made him quit, all the while knowing he was working on becoming an Eagle Scout. He missed his scout leader and friends, and all the fun trips where he could get away from home and be a kid.

He had certainly not grown up with the love and encouragement that surrounded me growing up. But in spite of it, he excelled in school, in college, and found a wonderful job in the lumber industry as a sales rep right out of college. He bought his first house at twenty-one years old!

He was definitely an overcomer and overachiever, but also humble. I liked that combination! I believed he was someone on whom I could depend.

Gary and I talked more about God and the important role He had played in my life; how I had backslidden over the past five years; how I had been riding the fence with one foot on God's side with the other on the world's side.

I told him how I had prayed that God would send me someone strong, a man on whom I could depend, and that I had even had made a list of qualities I wanted in that man, and had laid them before the Lord. One of the things on my list that was most important to me was this: that I be with someone who loved God and also wanted to place his life in

His hands, as I had recently done after trying to do life on my own, riding the fence, and failing miserably. And so very vital: that he accept and love my children.

Gary told me he believed in God and wanted to have that same trust I had experienced. He also explained that he thought there were many religions and that every one of them thought *their way* was the right one. I shared many scriptures with him and my experiences with Jesus, going all the way back to when I was a little girl.

I was praying that Gary would come to see very quickly the truth of this passage in the Gospel of John, where Jesus had declared:

John 14:6 (NIV)

⁶ ... "I am the way and the truth and the life. No one comes to the Father except through me."

But there was a growth period Gary had to go through for him to really trust God with his life. Up to this point he had basically made it on his own with very little help from anyone.

I reminded him that God had been watching over him his entire life, keeping him safe, giving him caring friends, his grandma, his coaches and scout leaders, and, of course, blessing him with his precious daughter, Brei. He agreed.

His journey with God began as he, too, needed to jump off of his fence into Jesus' arms and out of the world's clutches. We decided we would need to find a church to attend.

It had just been Gary and me up to this point (for five weeks), but it became time for him to meet my children and for me to meet his daughter, Brei. We decided a night out with the girls would be just the ticket (Matt had other plans). We chose miniature golfing, believing it would be fun. We met at the local Family Fun Center, chose our weapons (golf clubs and balls) and headed to the course.

The girls giggled and hit it off right away. Brei had been raised with a strict mom and had been told to be seen and not heard, so she was calm and a bit shy. Abby, on the other hand, was a free spirit, *very* active, and never sat still. She was running all over the little golf course and balls were flying everywhere. I told her firmly that it was time to calm down and behave before someone got hurt. Thankfully she behaved (well, kind of), and at least the balls stopped flying, but she never stopped moving and investigating everything, even the stream running through the course which left her with soaking socks and shoes! Brei did her best to keep up, and this would become the norm for them: Abby never stopping and Brei asking her, "When can we sit down and rest?"

Matt, too, met Gary and was relieved to see he wasn't wearing cowboy boots or refereeing soccer games. He could see we were both crazy about each other and that we all would be spending a lot of time together. He told me that Gary seemed like a good guy. Matt wanted me to be happy and taken care of.

Matt always possessed good discernment. I can remember friends from high school calling him for advice and Matt counseling them for hours on the phone. I, too, would request his take on various matters, and his advice was solid. I was happy he approved of Gary!

My parents had planned a trip for us (Matt, Abby, and me), using their timeshare for us to join them on the island of Kauai, as our Christmas gift. It was a lovely two-bedroom, two-bathroom condo in which we would be staying. We were to be gone for a week. Upon learning of these plans, Gary asked if there was any possible way that he and Brei could also join us. He had already met my folks, had enjoyed dinner at their house, and they had found him to be a very nice, and accomplished man. I had also told them how I was head-over-heels-crazy about him; I related the story behind us meeting, the list I had presented to God, wanting to get right again with the Lord, breaking it off with Cowboy (whom they loved), and feeling that Gary was my forever partner.

They agreed that he and Brei could come along to Hawaii, and Gary bought their plane tickets. The girls were *so* excited and Matt was along for the ride, watching and carefully discerning this new family dynamic.

We had a great time and mom bought the girls matching Hawaiian dresses and put them in a hula class at the resort. She loved fussing over them. Because Brei's grandmas lived out of town, she relished my mom's attention and immediately called my folks 'Grandmom' and 'Pop Pop'. They loved that and took Brei under their wings and treated her like one of their own grandkids.

One evening, Gary, Matt, and I took the rental van and went out to a fun luau where Gary was called up on stage to learn how to dance the hula … that was a hoot! Gary and I wanted to spend some special moments with Matt, as well. Matt enjoyed it all, and the three of us had a great time. Mom and dad stayed with the girls who basically collapsed every night about 7:00 p.m. after being up all day going non-stop: in the pool, in the ocean, snorkeling, swimming, etc. We all got along. It was a comfortable family dynamic and it just felt right.

I hadn't been this happy and content in a long time. I prayed, "Thank You, Lord, for answered prayer, for showing me how my life was best in Your hands, not mine or the world's clutches which had absolutely nothing to offer but pain and grief with a brief moment of pleasure."

Chapter 16
SURPRISE, SURPRISE, SURPRISE!

Gary and I had only been seeing each other for about six weeks but it seemed like months, and we were already talking about "forever!" Christmas was right around the corner and as was our usual family tradition, my folks would come over on Christmas morning to open gifts with us and later in the day we would gather at their home or one of my brothers' homes for the Christmas feast; each of us would bring a specialty dish.

Gary and Brei wanted to be included in all of it, so they stayed over on Christmas Eve, after our Christmas Eve party, so they could be involved with the opening of gifts on Christmas morning and dinner later in the day.

The girls were up fairly early and anxious to rip open their gifts. We let them each open one on Christmas Eve and told them they had to wait for Grandmom and Pop Pop to open gifts in the morning. They had some breakfast, my folks arrived, and the mayhem began. There were lots of excited cheers and happy faces as gifts were torn open.

I waded through the sea of wrapping paper to retrieve the gift Gary had bought me. Gary's gift was new snow skies, with poles and boots to follow once I was fitted for them. "WOW!" I thought it was an extravagant gift, as did the kids and my folks, by the looks on their faces. But that was not all.

He stood up in front of the Christmas tree and read a little speech he had prepared. He then asked me to marry him in front of my parents and the kids. *__Surprise!__* **(# 1)** It was more liked *shocked!* He had a beautiful diamond ring his jeweler friend had designed and opened the little box to present it to me. I jumped up without hesitation, hugged him, and said, "Yes!"

Suddenly Brei ran crying and locked herself in the bathroom; everyone else just sat there in disbelief. Abby asked, "Does this mean you're getting married? When?" When the shock started to wear off, there were hugs all around and Gary went into the bathroom to talk to Brei and comfort her. He assured her that she was still his number one girl and nothing would change his love for her, that this union would be the start of a loving family which she would now be a part of.

My mom secretly asked me, "Did you have any idea he was going to ask you to marry him? It's so soon." I explained that we had fallen in love quickly and were already committed to each other, but that I did not expect a marriage proposal. It was quite a surprise and quite frankly, I, too, was stunned!

Over the next month or so we talked about where, what, and when this marriage should occur. We questioned important questions: "Where should we all live? At his house, my house, or a new house? What type of wedding do we want to plan? Family only, big, small, or elope to Vegas? And when? How long should we wait?" We considered that we needed more time to "blend" our families and all get to know each other better.

Everything seemed to be moving at warp speed. We were going back and forth from house to house weekly. It was decided (and the decision came too quickly; I know that now...), for us to move into Gary's much nicer and bigger home with the bay view and swimming pool. We decided we would rent my house out to pay the monthly mortgage. This would mean putting Abby into a new elementary school down the hill from Gary's home. Matt was driving and would remain at his high school with his friends and sports. Brei would continue to come on the weekends and she and Abby would share a bedroom. Yep, we appeared to be one big, happy, blended family.

We were in love and engaged with marriage on the horizon, so I justified us living together since I felt myself climbing back onto the fence, and I was pleading my case to God. I hoped, surely, that He would understand. But deep inside I knew the scripture; I was feeling guilt and shame living this way in front of our children. What kind of example were we setting?

I knew and recalled this scripture:

Hebrews 13:4 (ESV)

4 Let marriage be held in honor among all, and let the marriage bed be undefiled, for God will judge the sexually immoral and adulterous.
The Holy Bible, English Standard Version. ESV® Text Edition: 2016. Copyright © 2001 by Crossway Bibles, a publishing ministry of Good News Publishers.

Abby was feeling scared sleeping in a new room, and in a new house, going to a new school with new friends. We set up a mat and sleeping bag along my side of the bed on the floor where she would sleep just about every night after waking up scared. Brei and Abby got along most of the time but if there were any outside friends in the mix, there was jealousy and fighting. Brei also reminded Abby that Gary was *her* daddy not Abby's dad, and she told me that her mom was clear that she should never call me 'mom,' that she only had one mom. Message received.

Matt was into high school life, sports, his buddies, and lots of girlfriends! He was also very independent, had a part time job, and his own car. He actually got his first job when he was thirteen: sweeping floors and stocking shelves at the neighborhood mini-mart. A nice couple owned the place and Matt and his friends would buy cokes and goodies in their store. The owner took a liking to Matt, who was always polite and respectful, and gave him a little "under the counter" job. He was thrilled to have his own spending money. But now in high school, he worked at a yogurt shop.

His friends would come over and hang by the pool, and he and Gary got along for the most part. He did not like Gary giving him orders. And there was certainly some resentment and anger displayed when he was told to pick up his mess or help out. I, of course, was placed in the middle. I became the mediator/referee; on the one hand, trying to protect my kids but also feeling I wasn't respecting Gary which ended in heated arguments between Gary and me.

I couldn't help but think we had jumped the gun in moving in together, putting stress on our children, as well as ourselves. We needed a break. My parents continued to be a constant in the kid's lives, and we were grateful they agreed to stay with them for a week while we took a trip to Maui for some rest and relaxation. It was lovely and restful, but when we returned home, something was off, way off.

We no sooner put our luggage down and mom and dad had left, that Matt said he had to talk to us right away and was obviously upset and nervous. He squirmed as he told us: one of the girls he had dated a few months ago was pregnant. She was sixteen, he was seventeen and they were no longer together. **_Surprise!_ (# 2)** Shock! Sadness! Shame! Stupid! How could he have let this happen? But, how could I have been so blind to see that the example I had provided to my teenage son over the past five years was so very wrong?! Was I really expecting the "do as I say, not as I do" to be heard?

They both had kept it a secret from Gary and me and the girl's parents for many months now, and decisions had to be made. Abortion was out. They were just kids. So, the best option was adoption. I talked on the phone with the girl's mother about what we and the kids thought was best, and that we had decided on adoption. They were too young to be parents; they were both still in school, and they weren't even together anymore. Her mother refused to put the baby up for adoption and said they would raise the baby, along with their daughter, as their own. She said she understood that Matt was just a kid and they didn't want him involved at all in the baby's life. The young girl dropped out of school, had the baby, and soon after her parents moved them all out of state.

Fast forward twenty years. Matt's son, our grandson, is in our lives off and on, and Matt and his son have a relationship. Matt's three children consider the young man to be their brother; they love him, and he loves them. God is good!

We were all busy with our day-to-day lives, doing our best to live together as a family. Matt graduated from high school, I placed Abby in the School for Creative and Performing Arts (she loved to dance and sing), and Brei was an "A" student and excelled in school.

Our first year together was drawing to a close and still no wedding! The conviction to marry and make our union right in God's eyes was heavy on my heart. It had been a tough year of transition, so I inquired frequently to Gary if he still wanted to get married. He always said, "Yes, honey, whatever you want to do; I'm on board." The ball was squarely placed in my court and I chose to run with it!

My friend and mentor, Lisa, and I went to the gym at lunch time three times a week. After our aerobics class, our lunch spot was a cheap but yummy fast food Mexican restaurant. Gary's 40th birthday was coming up on December 17 (also Brei's birthday), and I wanted to plan a surprise party for him. As we started to list the people I wanted to invite to Gary's birthday party, I realized it was the same list of people I wanted to invite to our wedding.

Lisa suggested that we just get married at his party. I responded, "What if we kept it *all* a surprise?" In other words, he wouldn't know about the birthday party *or* the wedding until he showed up! It was just over a month out, and we had work to do!

I went down to the County Recorder's office to see if I could even pull this off. I was told that if I could find a Pastor who was also a certified public accountant and would agree to do the wedding without Gary's knowledge, it could be done. The clerk gave me a list of those names. I contacted a Reverend S. and met with him, told him our story, and he agreed to do the wedding. I rushed to pick up blank invitations, wrote the invite which included at the bottom: "Shhhh … this is a complete surprise to Gary!" I arranged for the invitations to be printed, and requested that all RSVPs would be called in to Lisa. They were in the mail in a few days. Our friends, Judy and Rick, lived in a lovely home with a large deck overlooking a beautiful canyon, and they agreed we could have the wedding there.

RSVPs were coming in like crazy and most would ask, "Is the wedding also a surprise to Gary?" Lisa had a grand time responding, "Yes, it is, so be sure not to say anything to him." His guy friends were particularly uncomfortable with the whole deal and I had to threaten them within an inch of their lives to stay quiet or die!

Abby and Brei would be my bridesmaids in their velvet red dresses, Lisa my bridesmaid in her red dress, and Matt would walk me down the aisle, or onto the deck. It was December 17, so everything was decorated in red and white poinsettias. A red runner was placed on the floor leading from inside the house up to the archway out on the deck, where we would stand to be married. The archway was also decorated in red and white flowers. Lisa had ordered the food, wine, and champagne; all was delivered before we arrived. My dear friend, Audrey, would sing, "Somewhere In Time," and another friend would be playing the piano as I walked out. I had already taken over my dress, the girl's dresses, and Gary's tux, red cummerbund and bow tie, the day before. I had to grab his dress shoes on the way out the door and wrap them in a towel. He thought we were going over to Judy and Rick's for a simple BBQ, to celebrate his birthday. **<u>Surprise! (# 3)</u>**

I had even contacted Gary's mom and step dad to tell them of my plan, and they agreed to drive out to San Diego from Oklahoma for the wedding. I had never met them since they had moved from San Diego before Gary and I were together. We had only spoken on the phone. I asked my parents if they could stay at their house, and they agreed. This was one more surprise for Gary to cope with. They would also stay with the kids while Gary and I took a 3-day mini-honeymoon in San Diego which I had planned. This included staying at the historic Hotel Del Coronado.

Everything had come together, no one let the cat out of the bag, and we were headed over to Judy and Rick's. Matt had gotten there early and parked everyone's car out of the cul-de-sac where they lived so when we arrived, we were the only car to park out front. Our friend, Owen, was perched at the front window with the video camera rolling through a crack in the curtain, along with his comedic commentary: "Little does he know that when he walks through the door his life will change forever; poor guy."

There were 60+ friends and family in attendance! Gary's mom was standing front and center when the door was opened and everyone yelled, "Surprise!" His mom hugged him and he looked so confused and was obviously having an out of body experience, trying to piece it together: "Why would all these people (some from out of town) be here for a 40th birthday party?" The back of his shirt was damp with sweat as people high-fived and hugged him.

It quieted down and I said, "There is someone here I'd like you to meet." The group parted and up walked Reverend S. Gary looked even more confused, not knowing who he was. I said, "This is Reverend S., and if it's okay with you, he's going to marry us today."

You could hear a pin drop. Gary replied, "I couldn't think of a better time," and suddenly everything made sense to him as the cheers erupted. He gave me a big hug and kiss and we all made our way back into separate bedrooms to dress for the ceremony. Gary couldn't believe I had taken his tux and shoes and had kept all of this a secret for over a month!

It was a happy, glorious celebration which included three cakes … our wedding cake, a birthday cake for Gary, and another birthday cake for Brei. Every year for 31 years as of this writing, we celebrate these three wonderful occasions together. On some years it has been harder than others as we faced life together with its ups and downs, valleys, and mountain tops.

Riding the Fence Really Hurts!

I was just so happy to have both feet back on solid ground and focused on doing life God's way, whatever it took, with no more compromises. Knowing I was finally in a right relationship which God had coordinated with Gary, I was excited to be obedient once again and to be using my gifts and talents for God's glory.

I wanted us all to grow together in our faith and for Gary and I to become good examples to our children. I would boldly tear down the fence I had been riding, and never climb up and ride it again. **Never!**

> I was just so happy to have both feet back on solid ground and focused on doing life God's way, whatever it took, with no more compromises.

Chapter 17
GROWING PAINS

I remember growing up that I would get terrible leg pain from all of the dancing, and being put into ballet shoes at seven years old. My little legs just couldn't take all the stress and strain, and they would ache. My mom would rub them with alcohol and the pain would ease, and then I could sleep. But even with the anticipated pain, I would not quit my dance classes and the thrill that came from performing.

I had performed throughout my life on multiple stages and rode a fence on and off for years. Now, with a new life of no longer riding that fence, together with my husband, we experienced major growing pains.

Gary and I both had past lives to deal with. We had both been married twice. As hard as we tried to not carry our pasts into our present, we did bring some baggage with us into our marriage. Me with never wanting to be under anyone's control ever again, knowing I could make it on my own, and him with trust issues due to two wives who had cheated on him many times.

We were also dealing with kid issues and everyone getting along in a pureed and blended family. I felt like I needed to be constantly defending my children and Gary felt disrespected when I didn't side with him.

Another "surprise" came when Matt, now 20, who had been dating a gal for a while, came to us with the news that they were expecting a baby. He wanted to marry the mother of their child but she decided to go back to her former boyfriend. Precious Paige was born and we were all there to greet her and welcome her with open arms. Matt was a doting father from day one and has been a constant presence in her life from diapers to pig tails, to cheer uniforms, to marriage. Paige (age 28 in 2021) and her husband, just blessed us with our first great grandchild, Amelia Rose.

My job at the rock and roll station, KGB, consisted of finding new clients, servicing existing clients, and keeping their advertising on the air. This meant getting results for the clients and the station, often writing scripts for the commercials with our production department. This interface also included entertaining these clients. So, I arranged for frequent lunches out with these clients (many of them were men). These constant promotional events kept me out and about—a lot. I would find myself explaining over and over again to Gary that I was totally committed to our marriage, deeply in love with him, asking him to trust me. I would invite him to promotions so he could experience these efforts firsthand and hopefully better understand the responsibilities that came with my job.

Our social life had become a struggle when we would be invited to parties with Gary's friends. They were drinkers and acted inappropriately when they drank alcohol. I didn't drink, but would watch as their drinking took affect and then took over. These nights would regularly end in an argument about me being too friendly while singing around a piano, or talking to a guy. All of this was alcohol-abuse-driven. This became a wake-up call. I concluded that things had to change. While that old fence was gone, never to return, I was determined to stay firmly placed within God's plan.

I would claim this awesome verse:

James 1:12 (NIV)

"Blessed is the one who perseveres under trial because, having stood the test, that person will receive the crown of life that the Lord has promised to those who love him."

My prayer during these times was succinct: "Dear Lord, Thank You for giving me the strength to endure trials and tribulations. I may feel weak, but I will continue to put my trust in You. You always make a way."

> "Dear Lord, Thank You for giving me the strength to endure trials and tribulations. I may feel weak, but I will continue to put my trust in You.
> <u>You always make a way</u>."

As I did with each challenge now, I laid these "growing pains" daily before the Lord, asking Him to keep me focused on Him and Him alone, while seeking His wisdom and discernment. As with my earlier dance classes, I wasn't about to quit because of some "growing pains." My unequivocal choice was this: I will *not* lose faith in God's plan. I knew the pains, physical and sociological, were temporary and could be healed.

The truth about the alcohol issue came to me clearly. I explained to Gary that our marriage was not strong enough at this time to continue attending these parties. I was uncomfortable in going and the results regularly ended badly. In all honesty, I told him that I was fine with him going alone since they were mostly his friends, but that I wouldn't be going with him any longer.

I had anticipated another argument coming, but he said he understood and agreed. He never attended another party. Instead, we scheduled date nights and finally decided to go to the church my son had started attending (a huge answer to prayer). It was a bit of a hike from our house, but the teaching was wonderful and the worship music simply glorious. Being there with my son and some other friends was the icing on the cake!

Boy, was I glad to be back in church! With tears streaming down my cheeks as I sang, I felt the Holy Spirit washing over me! I could hear God saying, "Welcome back; we've missed you." The prodigal daughter had returned home to a beautiful celebration of love and forgiveness.

In between these growing pains Gary and I decided we wanted to rebuild our house. He worked hand-in-hand with a budding architect. During reconstruction, we moved down the street, renting a house for six and a half months as our house was rebuilt/remodeled. At the conclusion of the remodel, we moved back into this newly remodeled home. Whew, this adventure had been a huge endeavor and lots of work, but it was well worth it.

The extra space, an upstairs master suite and family room, was a true blessing! God's blessings were falling on us like a spring rain. Never in my wildest dreams did I ever think I'd live in a home like this. God had brought me from low rental apartments to a gorgeous home. I was so full of gratitude and thankfulness for God's loving care and abundant blessings.

A life lesson: When we surrender in obedience to what God is calling us to do, and truly turn our lives over to His care, He blesses us beyond what "we could ask or imagine ..." Ephesians 3:20 (NIV)

> A life lesson: When we surrender in obedience to what God is calling us to do, and truly turn our lives over to His care, He blesses us beyond what "we could ask or imagine ..." Ephesians 3:20 (NIV)

Our girls were entering high school. Abby decided to leave the School of Creative and Performing Arts and attend the local high school so she could cheer and be with her local friends. She had taken a bus to the performing arts school from the 4th-8th grade, and had been in many performances, using her amazing gifts and talents, but she wanted a change. She started at our local high school in the 9th grade and soon was bored, even with cheering, but hung in there and graduated from that school.

She attended the local City College, majoring in the fine arts/dance program. She continued to perform and it was always a thrill to watch these performances. This led to her teaching dance to children and also hip hop at an after-school program at a local high school. The pay was poor, so she ended up in the hospitality industry for many years as a concierge. She is now an "Elder Exercise Specialist," has her own business, and teaches at a beautiful retirement community in La Jolla, California.

Brei was in a charter school which offered many extra-curricular classes like photography, ceramics, dance, yearbook, auto shop, and theater, along with advanced scholastic classes. She loved it and couldn't wait to get off to college and out from under the control of her domineering mother. Eventually she would be accepted into Manhattan College, a private college in New York. She graduated from this college with a double major in communications and industrial phycology. Her career has skyrocketed, and she is now a Director of Human Resources for a local pharmaceutical company.

In the mid-90s we heard about a local youth pastor, Miles McPherson, who was preaching at a nearby church, "Horizon Christian Fellowship," every Sunday evening, for two services. He conducted these two services back-to-back in an effort to accommodate the amazing crowds who were pouring in, mostly young people. We encouraged our girls to join us, and they did on occasion.

Miles was a former NFL player with quite a testimony and a true gift of exhortation. He was also hilarious; but he preached the Word with conviction and sincerity. People were getting saved week after week. It was very exciting!

We started attending every Sunday night instead of driving to our former church so far away on Sunday morning. I knew I would need to start volunteering and getting involved. Then it was announced one Sunday evening that Miles had felt the call to start a new church and was given the blessing of the senior pastor at Horizon to move on and follow God's calling. Gary and I knew right away that we would follow him and be a part of this new worship venture, the Rock Church, San Diego.

I could hardly wait to get involved with ministry at this rapidly growing church. I started by becoming an altar call counselor, talking and praying with people who came forward at the end of the sermon. But in my heart, I really wanted to start a women's Bible study group and teach. I was interviewed by a woman overseeing this ministry (in-home "life groups") and was told I wasn't quite ready to teach, and to continue doing the altar call counseling. At first my ego was hurt, but I realized she was right. I started going to Bible studies with two women who were amazing teachers and they taught me much about leading and serving.

This was a huge time of spiritual growth for me. I became involved with their ministry and helped them with marketing and retreats. They gave me the opportunity to teach breakout groups at their retreats and this empowered me to use my gift of teaching. Soon I was back interviewing with someone new, overseeing "life groups," and was encouraged to start a women's "life group" (Bible study) in my home! I could hardly wait to start!

I was doing great with my radio career and making money that I didn't even know was possible! Gary was excelling in his career as the General Manger of the wholesale lumber operation. But my ongoing question to him, since I was now using my gifts and talents volunteering with the church, was

Riding the Fence Really Hurts!

this: "How do you want to use your gifts and talents, could you start volunteering and become involved?"

I would encourage him to build houses in Tijuana, Mexico, help with a building project at the church, go to the men's retreat and attend weekly Bible studies, etc. I would leave articles for him to read, and my Bible open to scriptures I wanted him to see. I couldn't understand why he wasn't stepping up like I was, because I was feeling led to do these things, to serve.

I would soon be "schooled" in the differences between nagging vs. offering uplifting encouragement. I began allowing God to do the work in my husband. This was a lesson which lifted a burden from me, giving me freedom and counsel, which I then would pass on, to the many women that God was bringing into my life!

> I began allowing God to do the work in my husband. This was a lesson which lifted a burden from me, giving me freedom and counsel, which I then would pass on, to the many women that God was bringing into my life!

Chapter 18
BIKER BARS, BIBLE STUDIES, AND BUILDING

Her name was Norma: a gifted, funny, high spirited, elegantly dressed speaker at a convention we attended with my son for his online business. She and her husband, Joe, had led a pretty sordid past before surrendering their lives to God. They had owned a biker bar, dealt in drugs, and Joe was even jailed in Tijuana, Mexico at one time.

What was that all about? Looking at this woman you would have never guessed this had been her past, but you could quickly see she loved sharing the journey, and she was good at telling her story. It had been a story of despair, anger, and destruction that eventually had brought her into a life of redemption, peace, and freedom.

She told one story of a woman coming into the biker bar and cozying up to Joe at the bar. She let it slide, all the while shooting Joe disapproving glares that he seemed to be ignoring since he was enjoying the attention way too much! She could feel the anger bubbling up inside her (an ongoing problem she had to deal with), and her mind was reeling with how to handle the situation.

She concluded that the only way to handle this was the old school, "biker rules." She went into the back room and came back with a shotgun, pointed it at Joe and the woman sitting at the bar and said, "Get away from my husband. It's time for you to go ... now!" Joe jumped up, everyone scattered, and the woman ran out. This was just one of several stories she would tell us. She had led a tough life and no one messed with her.

But then, "Jesus!" She and Joe became churchgoing believers and Norma embraced this life with all that high-spirited energy and enthusiasm God had blessed her with, but this time for His glory! She hit the ground running, going to Bible studies, joining women's retreats, volunteering at the church, reading her Bible and daily devotionals. She couldn't get enough of the new life and freedom she had found in trusting Christ. But, she pondered, "Why wasn't Joe getting on board and excited to do the same?"

This next part of her story was a piece where it seemed like I was the only one in the audience listening, that she was talking directly to me. She went on to say that she kept encouraging Joe to volunteer, read his Bible, go to men's groups, etc., and he wasn't doing any of it! In fact, he would tell her to leave him alone and that old, familiar anger would resurface in her.

She brought her anger and frustration to the Lord in prayer, asking Him why He hadn't changed Joe's heart and made him into the Christian man she wanted? Boy, did that sound familiar! I was praying that same prayer about my husband, Gary.

The answer she received back from God was just what I needed to hear: "Leave Joe to me. I know his heart, his struggles, and talents; I don't need your help. Your timing is not mine. Just focus on Me and being the best wife, mother, friend, Christian, you can be, using *your* gifts and talents to complete the assignments I have for you, and when you're perfect, I'll let you know."

Ahh! It all made sense. Another burden was lifted. I would move forward, following God's lead, teaching, counseling, volunteering where I felt led, and would leave my loving husband in the capable hands of God.

This word from God revolutionized our married life. Gary became supportive (and still is) of anything I felt God was calling me to do. His call has included Bible studies in our home, counseling, women's retreats, opening two homes for recovering women and children and running them for almost five years, teaching Bible Studies to teens in Juvenile Hall, and most recently helping women come out of human trafficking.

The Rock Church purchased a local strip joint, called, "The Body Shop," shut it down, and in 2021 renovations started. This once disgusting place (for 50 years a strip club) will become "The Freedom Center," a place for women who have experienced human trafficking, to come for refuge, counseling, transitional living, help in finding jobs or schooling, and the hope that comes from trusting their heavenly Father with their lives. I'm serving on the steering committee! God is *good*!

After 26 years in the lumber industry, the company Gary had worked for was shut down. Gary was 45 years old and decided to get his general contractor's license.

I had taken a job as the National Sales Manager for the KFMB stations (two) in San Diego and was being paid well. This gave Gary time to study, do some small contracting jobs, and then excel as a licensed general contractor for the next twenty years.

I was at the KFMB stations for almost five years, and then felt led to leave and take a local sales manager position with a Christian operated radio company.

My son, Matt, had been working for them in sales for a few years and encouraged me to come over and work for this large Christian organization that owned 100 stations nationwide. I took a cut in pay but knew it was the right choice. This was the year 2000.

After one year as the local sales manager for the new news/talk station, our general manager decided to go on the air full time as our morning show host (his love and background was as an announcer), and he recommended to the CEO that I take over the role as the station's General Manager (GM).

After several interviews, I was put into the GM position. I was the only female GM for the company at that time. This was *all* God!

WOW! God surprised me with that move. Never had I thought back in 1987 when I interviewed for my first sales job at KGB radio, that I would someday be placed in a general manager's position overseeing all the operations of two radio stations.

Tasks included putting budgets together, overseeing health plans, hiring, firing, learning *all* the operations of a radio station, including how radio towers worked and what it meant when our news/talk tower had to be moved (and I was responsible to help find a new location for our new tower).

Many hours were spent with our engineer and corporate; these hours included speaking in front of the City Council to get it all approved. This approval included local neighbors signing off on having a radio tower in their area. I can truly say it is by the grace of God this was approved!

Again, a scripture came to mind:

Ephesians 3:20-21 (NKJV)

[20] Now to Him who is able to do exceedingly abundantly above all that we ask or think, according to the power that works in us, [21] to Him *be* glory in the church by Christ Jesus to all generations, forever and ever. Amen.
Scripture taken from the New King James Version®. Copyright © 1982 by Thomas Nelson. Used by permission. All rights reserved.

During my time as the General Manager, I was blessed with a mentor who taught me all phases of leadership, how to place people in their proper positions, guiding us in writing our vision and mission statements for our stations with our management staff, and how good leaders lead. Thank you, Glen Aubrey, Creative Team Resources Group (www.ctrg.com), for your endless time and energy in working with me and our team! We will always remain good friends.

I would remain as the GM until April, 2006, when I felt God opening yet another door and opportunity to grow. I took a position at The Rock Church as the Marketing and Communications Director. Even though this position lasted only for a short seven months, due to a change in CEOs and new leadership's desire to re-position people and make changes, it was a wonderful experience working with gifted

Riding the Fence Really Hurts!

people. I knew that if God wanted me to remain in that job, a team of wild horses couldn't drag me out! It was certainly a test in trust and humility. What was God up to now?

It was the first time I didn't have another job lined up to go to. However, Gary's general contracting business was successful and thriving, so we were fine financially.

I was reminded of my prayer from two years earlier when, exhausted from the GM position, I asked God, "Lord, I've been working since I was seventeen. I'm tired, and ready to do whatever You have planned, but when can I have a rest?"

God led me to The Rock, another demanding position, and then knowing His perfect plan for me in ministry, took me out and told me to "…lie down in green pastures; He leadeth me beside the still waters. He restoreth my soul …" (Psalm 23, KJV).
The King James Version of the Holy Bible (KJV). The KJV is in the public domain.

Thank you, Jesus. The next week I was rollerblading almost every day on the beach boardwalk! I enjoyed having coffee with friends at locations overlooking the ocean, walking on the beach, and having intimate talks with my Jesus. I was being restored. It was glorious!

Matthew 11:28 (NIV)

²⁸"Come to me, all you who are weary and burdened, and I will give you rest."

Blessings and rewards come with obedience. God is a good, good, Father!

> Blessings and rewards come with obedience.

Chapter 19
OKAY, NOW WHAT?

I was really embracing this life of freedom and thanking God for it, but I knew there was something else for which God was preparing me. I did some marketing for various friends, freelanced with the Christian radio company as a part-time sales rep at their request, working from home, and was loving teaching the weekly women's Bible study which was growing.

I had the opportunity while working for the Rock church to participate in an in-depth course in Christian Counseling, being offered through the American Association of Christian Counselors, AACC. After completing the course, I was certified by the AACC as a Certified Biblical Counselor. My thought was that I could offer Christian counseling at a very reasonable rate, or if needs be, at no charge for those without the capability to pay.

I even got business cards printed, and registered for a business license. A couple of clients were referred to me; one paid for two sessions, and the other was a phone counseling situation (out of state), and he never paid!

It became perfectly clear that this was to be my ministry with no fees attached, and that God would bless it and supply our needs. Here it is fifteen years later with numerous counseling sessions that continue weekly, and believe me when I say, God has supplied *all* our needs and much more!

I continued to enjoy my walks on the beach, sometimes with friends or with women I was counseling. My coffee spot overlooking the beach, Kono's Coffee, became my "outdoor counseling office." I found it therapeutic to meet counselees there, outside, watching the waves crash, the birds soar, and experience the sand between our toes. We were taking in all the magnificence of God's creation, knowing these times and this place were His, and part of His plan.

Psalm 139:17,18 (NIV)

[17] How precious to me are your thoughts, God! How vast is the sum of them! [18] Were I to count them, they would outnumber the grains of sand—when I awake, I am still with you.

One of my long-time friends, Tami, often walked with me and we would sit on the sand and pray for her daughter who was using drugs and who also was enduring psychological issues. This condition would cause the daughter to act out and be a danger to herself. My friend and her husband had a real burden for women suffering from drug addiction and the children being raised by these women.

Riding the Fence Really Hurts!

They talked about moving out of their two-story home and renting it to an organization that would use it as a Christian rehab home for recovering women and children. They were counseling with a Christian Marriage and Family Therapist (MFT), Damaris, also an RN, and shared this idea with her. Damaris had started a 501 (c) 3 non-profit. She also had a burden to open a restoration home for women and children, but she needed someone with administrative skills to help her run it. I told my friend that their home should be called **Natalie's House of Grace**. The home was named after Natalie, her daughter. We cried and knew God had put a plan in place!

We called together a group of Godly, praying women, and gathered around a table on the deck at Kono's Coffee overlooking the ocean. After much discussion, laughter, prayers and tears, a plan was put in place and in motion. Damaris would be the Director and I would be the Administrator of **Natalie's House of Grace** which would be under the umbrella of the non-profit already in place. Natalie would be our first resident. Many more would come after her. I was now in fulltime ministry and loving it!

We watched as lives were restored through programs we had in place, and by the grace of God, these women surrendered their lives to Christ. Children under Child Protective Services (CPS), were returned to their mothers. Some of the women went back to college. Others found jobs and moved out and went on with their lives. However, some weren't ready or willing to do the work and, sadly, returned to their addictions or abuse.

Another home was opened when my friend and her husband decided to sell **Natalie's House of Grace** after a couple of years. The new home was called **Jessica's House of Hope**, named after one of the women who, with two small boys, had excelled in our program. We also had a missionary friend, April, who moved to the Philippines and opened a home under our non-profit umbrella. This home was for women and children in another country, and this answered the question of why God had moved Damaris to add the label, "international" as part of the name of the non-profit years before. God knew what the future would hold!

We ran the homes for almost five years when the second house was also put up for sale. There were only a couple gals left, and they were ready to move on, so we knew God was closing things down. We continued to pray God would bring another home but this was not to be. That season of our lives had come and gone; we were obedient to the daunting assignment God had placed before us. I will cherish this experience forever. I thank God for choosing me to step out in faith and rely on Him to guide, direct, mature in my faith, and trust in Him.

This time and circumstances included steps of faith and trust for Gary, too. He watched me navigate some scary situations as we relied on God to lead and protect. I was so thankful God had given me a husband who would love and support me, as well as provide me with sound wisdom and advice when needed.

Jesus' example to His disciples of being a servant, illustrated as He washed their dusty, dirty feet (recorded in John, Chapter 13) was really put to the test as we served these women and children, many of whom didn't want to be cleansed from the hurt, shame, and guilt which they carried.

But as we humbled ourselves, loved and served those God had brought our way, they came to know and understand the true love of their heavenly father. What a lesson for us to learn! God never gives up on anyone. His love and forgiveness are boundless!

> This verse rang true once again, this time for those I was serving …
>
> Romans 8:38, 39 (NIV)
>
> ³⁸ For I am convinced that neither death nor life, neither angels nor demons, neither the present nor the future, nor any powers, ³⁹ neither height nor depth, nor anything else in all creation, will be able to separate us from the love of God that is in Christ Jesus our Lord.

> What a lesson for us to learn! God never gives up on anyone. His love and forgiveness are boundless!

It became time to take a deep breath and prepare for the assignments ahead of me. I was ready for a time of renewal and strength. The past five years had been hectic. I had been providing a lot of counseling for The Rock and had also continued to teach weekly.

As part of a yearly physical, I had scheduled my annual mammogram, and went in for the boob crushing! A few days later I received a phone call that would catch me off guard. I was told that I needed to go back in for a biopsy because a tiny tumor had been found. Another phone call came, this one telling me the biopsy had revealed a diagnosis: I had triple negative breast cancer and I needed to see an oncologist and surgeon right away. After that phone call, I sat stunned, trying to process what I'd been told.

My son, Matt, traditionally never dropped in during the day; but this day, right after that phone call, he came over to visit. I was still sitting at my computer having just received the cancer diagnosis. He walked in and I collapsed in his arms, telling him that I had breast cancer and I began to cry.

He reminded me of this truth: I was in God's care, and everything was going to be fine. He helped me understand that this was a trial we would get through, and that it would bring God glory. I hung onto Matt for dear life, desperately desiring to believe everything he was telling me. I thanked God for sending my son to me, and for the comfort God knew I would find in his embrace and words of wisdom.

I did intense research on chemo, integrated health care, and chose to go to the highly recommended clinic in San Diego for an alternative health regimen, Vitamin C, Turmeric IVs, and holistic care. I changed my diet: no sugar, little grains and dairy, and lots of green leafy veggies. I was also seeing my oncologist and my surgeon. The tumor was removed along with the surrounding margins, and a lymph node was also removed which thankfully had showed no cancer.

I declined chemo. This was a personal choice. This is not a recommendation for anyone else, in any way, shape, or form.

God was providing me with amazing, healing scriptures, and confirming my choices. This year was 2015. Everything appeared to go well and I believed I was good to go. Two years later the cancer was re-discovered in the same breast, a tiny tumor presenting as a pimple on the outside.

My surgeon confirmed it was the same triple negative cancer. I went in for another lumpectomy with margins removed and all went well this time, too. As before, I didn't move forward with chemo but did agree to receive targeted radiation for four weeks.

Judy Bowen

I endured *no* side effects and went on a ten-day river cruise just days after my radiation, feeling healthy and well, praising God for healing and restoration.

As of this writing, I have been cancer free for four years.

Here are just a few of the versus God revealed to me (all NIV):

Psalm 73:26

My flesh and my heart may fail, but God is the strength of my heart and my portion forever.

Malachi 4:2b

… the sun of righteousness will rise with healing in its rays …

Deuteronomy 31:6

[6] Be strong and courageous. Do not be afraid or terrified because of them, for the LORD your God goes with you; he will never leave you nor forsake you.

God uses each trial and test so we can help others. As I continue to counsel many women, God has continually positioned my life experiences to encourage others to trust Him, and to never give up regardless of the situation.

> God uses each trial and test so we can help others.

If we surrender to *His* will and plan for our lives, we can declare with confidence what Job had said: "Though he slay me, yet will I hope in him; I will surely defend my ways to his face." Job 13:15, NIV

> "Whatever happens is for His good purpose and for His glory, I am not afraid."
> ~ Francine Rivers, my favorite Christian novelist

Chapter 20
BUILDING A LEGACY

My son, Matt, had prayed for, and wrote a description of the woman he wanted to marry someday, and laid it before the Lord. God blessed him with a beautiful wife, Paty, who fulfilled everything in his descriptive prayer. They have blessed Gary and me with two grandchildren, Nicole and Matthew.

We love being grandparents to these two amazing children who are being trained up in the Lord, have accepted Him as their Savior, and have been baptized (their choice) in a Bible teaching church where they are very active. Matt's oldest daughter, Paige, age 28 as of this writing, has been an amazing big sister to Nicole and Matthew, and a loving granddaughter to us. As mentioned, she and her husband, Thomas, have just blessed us with a *great* grandchild, Amelia Rose. The family attended her dedication to the Lord on Easter Sunday, 2021. Our prayer is that she, too, will grow to love and serve the Lord.

Brei (my step-daughter) is engaged to a kind and generous man and they are raising our precious grandson, Brycen, who, as of this writing, is almost three years old. Our prayer is that he, too, will grow to know how much Jesus loves him and has an abundant plan for his life.

Brei's gift is generosity, and she freely gives to any in need. She loves her family fiercely, and her friends. But I believe she struggles to know how very much her heavenly Father loves her and wants to give her peace. We will continue to love her and pray for that "peace that passes understanding."

My daughter, Abby, is thriving after many, many years of living off and on that pesky fence. She has always had a deep belief in God, yet struggled with the tug of the world and finding peace and ongoing joy. Even in the midst of her struggles she would come to me for comfort and advice. We would sit and talk about how much Jesus loved her and wanted the very best for her. I had prayed for twenty years that she would fall to her knees and totally surrender to Him.

My prayers were answered when she told me, after a long night of drinking, that the following morning she literally fell to her knees and said, "Jesus, help me! I can't do this anymore." These were the words Jesus was waiting to hear, and they were the words I had prayed that she would offer to the Lord, so many times. She is currently nineteen months sober, has lost over 40 pounds, is focused on Christ and *His* plan for her life and she has met a wonderful man who adores

Riding the Fence Really Hurts!

her. She is finally at peace and I continue to thank God every day for answered prayer. Never stop praying and believing in God's miraculous healing!

This promise has given me comfort and proved to be very true:

Proverbs 22:6 (KJV)

Train up a child in the way he should go: and when he is old, he will not depart from it.

> Never stop praying and believing in God's miraculous healing!

Even in my wandering in and out of the world, on and off the fence, I always spoke to my children of Jesus and His love for us and the importance of trusting Him with our lives.

For the past 32 years they have watched my life and I have seen what God can do when we surrender completely to His leading and direction. From trials and valleys to victory and mountain top experiences, they have witnessed, in me, a "new life in Christ" and the contentment that comes from that life.

Psalm 37:4 (KJV)

> Delight thyself also in the LORD: and he shall give thee the desires of thine heart.

What is delight? "Delight" – something that gives great pleasure.
~Merriam-Webster Dictionary

The title of this chapter is "Building a Legacy." The word "legacy" means "something handed down."
~Merriam-Webster Dictionary

The question we all face is this: what is that "something" which we are handing down to our children, grandchildren, friends, or anyone with whom we interact?

Perhaps you, like me, have struggled to stay grounded on God's side of the fence. Continually feeling the tug of the world, you are listening to the enemy's lies: that you're missing out if you follow God's will for your life. Remember, Satan is a liar and a thief, stealing the abundant plan and the blessings God has in store for you.

Or perhaps you've never made the decision to jump off the fence and into the arms of your heavenly Father because your past has left you unable to trust parents and other people in your life who have disappointed you, were not there for you, even abused you.

Riding the Fence Really Hurts!

Please believe me when I say: your heavenly Father will never leave you or forsake you. He has you in the palm of His hand and will not let you go. You may think you're running away, or hiding from Him, but He's always there, waiting for you to come home into His loving arms.

It's never too late to start building your legacy and living life God's way.

> It's never too late to start building your legacy and living life God's way.

Here are some life changing lessons I've learned about the dismount from the fence. I actually picture myself as one of those amazing gymnasts landing the "Perfect 10 Dismounts," hands in the air, Praising God, and "sticking it!"

1. Don't settle for anything/anyone but God's best for you. If it doesn't feel right, *stop*, listen to that still small voice. God is protecting you.

2. Know what you want and what you don't want. Write down what you want, your vision, and read it often. Pray over it and leave it with the Lord, trusting Him with the outcome.

3. Know the difference between Satan's lies and God's truths. God's truths are the Fruit of the Spirit. Does

your situation and your relationships exhibit ... "love, joy, peace, longsuffering, kindness, goodness, faithfulness, gentleness, self-control?" (Galatians 5:22, 23a NKJV) If not, your situation and relationships are not from God.

Scripture taken from the New King James Version®. Copyright © 1982 by Thomas Nelson. Used by permission. All rights reserved.

I encourage you to pay close attention to this verse:

Colossians 2:8 (NIV)

See to it that no one takes you captive through hollow and deceptive philosophy, which depends on human tradition and the elemental spiritual forces of this world rather than on Christ.

4. Don't be embarrassed to seek wise counsel. Do this *before* things have gotten out of control. Sometimes we don't have the discipline to go to the scriptures and find answers, but there are counselors/therapists who have done this for you and can and will use God's Word (and should) to guide and direct you. We want and need to know what God says, not what our friends say that may agree with us instead of hurting our feelings with honesty and truth spoken in love. Remember that old saying: misery loves company.

5. Even when you're messing up, continue to pray and talk to God about everything. He's still listening and covets your prayers and time with you. He is still your heavenly Father and wants the best for you, His best!

6. When you've finally had enough of being kicked around by the world and all of the enemy's lies, find a Bible teaching church where you can sit quietly and soak in the music, the teaching, and the smiles; a church that embraces other flawed, but forgiven, believers.

7. Dust off your Bible and ask for the Holy Spirit's guidance as you consume the Word of God. Start with the Gospel of John, the fourth book of the New Testament. Read an encouraging devotion at the start of every day. There are many online that will come into your email box daily, or purchase ***Jesus Calling, God Calling*** or ***My Utmost for His Highest***; these are three amazing devotional books that you can mark up, and write personal notes in.

8. Join a small group that meets weekly and shares their lives, studies the Word, and prays for one another. Most churches have these groups that meet in homes or meet at the church. *Great* fellowship and new friends!

9. Find someone to whom you can be accountable, an "accountability partner." This is a person with whom you can share your ups and downs; send each other a scripture text or email daily. Share prayer requests.

A verse to encourage this kind of fellowship:

Proverbs 27:17 (NIV)

As iron sharpens iron, so one person sharpens another.

10. Serve! Find a ministry in which you can serve. Jesus' entire life exemplified serving others.

Matthew 20:26b (NIV)

…whoever wants to become great among you must be your servant, …

Until we start serving others, our name remains "Me, Me." In the absence of serving, we are focused on ourselves, consumed with our struggles, and our own lives. Serving sets us free, blesses others, and in turn truly blesses us!

> Serving sets us free, blesses others, and in turn truly blesses us!

Riding the Fence Really Hurts!

Being off the fence now for 32 years (wow, where do the years go?), I see the hand of God in everything. He's blessed my family, my finances, my career, my ministries, and continues to give me more amazing ways to serve Him.

I remember visiting my mom at the retirement community she and my dad moved into when my dad's Alzheimer's got too much for her to handle on her own. My dad got worse, and was eventually moved into a lovely home which cared for Alzheimer victims just up the street from the retirement community which left mom in a studio room by herself.

Weekly I would leave work and go to have lunch with mom in the beautiful Wesley Palms dining room. She loved introducing me to everyone and treating me to lunch. On one particular day, as I parked my car, I noticed one of the elderly residents sitting by herself on a bench; she looked so lonely and sad. I can remember saying to God, out loud, "Lord, please use me until the day I die; I don't ever want to be idle and alone sitting on a bench waiting for lunch. I'm all yours, surrendered to you 100%. Use me!"

My dad passed at age 83 after the long goodbye of ten years with Alzheimer's. Mom followed six years later at age 86 with severe dementia. My heart rejoices knowing they are at home with Jesus, laying their crowns at His feet.

I know we will all be together again for eternity! Now Gary and I are the matriarch/patriarch of our family. I'll be

70 later this year and God has not disappointed in fulfilling my request to be used!

"My cup runneth over" with ways to serve and minister to those in need. God is faithful and my desire to be faithful to Him, always.

A life lesson, to be sure:

> Psalm 71:17-18 (NIV)
>
> [17] Since my youth, God, you have taught me,
> and to this day
> I declare your marvelous deeds.
> [18] Even when I am old and gray, do not forsake
> me, my God, till   I declare your power to the
> next generation, your mighty acts to all who
> are to come.

I continue to teach the women's Bible Study in our home weekly; I'm counseling now, more than ever before. Being part of the prison ministry and teaching young girls about God's love in Juvenile Hall is an answer to prayer for me; it's something I've always wanted to do. It puts a smile on my face knowing God waited until I was a grandma to place me there.

Now the latest assignment and adventure is being a part of the **Freedom Center** (formerly the Bodyshop Strip Club), for

Riding the Fence Really Hurts!

victims of human trafficking. Center renovations will start soon and the center should be complete by early 2022. Many lives will be transformed and hope restored. That is an example of what Christ does through you and me, when we are willing to stand firmly on solid ground, obeying and serving, never to returning to "riding the fence."

> … an example of what Christ does through you and me,
> when we are willing to stand firmly on solid ground,
> obeying and serving,
> never to returning to "riding the fence."

Your Invitation

*****

If you have not yet asked Christ to be your Lord and Savior and you desire to invite Him into your life, or if you want to re-dedicate your whole life to Him, it's as easy as **ABC**.

I invite you to pray this prayer (Printed in The Rock Church Bulletin weekly):

1. "Father, I **Admit** I am a sinner and that my sin has brought death and destruction into my life, affecting my relationships with people, and my relationship with God. (Romans 3:23, 6:23)
2. "I **Believe** that Jesus died for my sins and that His death paid the penalty for my sins. (Romans 5:8)
3. "I **Confess** or agree that Jesus is Lord, that He died and rose from the dead, and He is able to forgive me of my sins. (Romans 10:9-10)

"Jesus, I trust that You love me and hear my prayer. By faith, I ask You to please forgive me and fill me with Your Holy Spirit. I surrender my life to You. I pray this in Jesus' name. Amen."

*****

Photo Gallery

Judy and Gary 50th Reunion, 2019

Photo Gallery

Judy Bowen, General Manager, 2000

Judy and Gary, January, 2012

Photo Gallery

Judy, Hawaii, 2019

Photo Gallery

Brei, Judy, Matt, and Abby, 2020

Closing Thoughts

Unfortunately, I wasted twenty years jumping on and off of the fence. While God continued to love me, bless me, and protect me and my children, I can't help think of how much peace I forfeited by being disobedient to what I knew God wanted and had planned for me. What I thought was going to make me happy made me fearful, ashamed, depressed, and disappointed.

Being off the fence now for 30+ years, focused on and seeking God's plan for my life, has been exciting to say the least! Using my gifts and talents to glorify God and help others, continues to be the most *amazing* personal blessing. Taking my eyes off myself, my selfish wants and desires, helping and serving others, fill my heart and soul with joy!

If you're still riding the fence, jump onto solid, firm ground, and stand unafraid, forgiven, and saved by grace, because you are God's masterpiece, "Fearfully and wonderfully made!" God's love gives you and me a new identity. We belong to Him!

Closing Thoughts

If you're still riding the fence,
      Jump onto solid, firm ground,
          Stand unafraid,
            Forgiven,
                Saved by grace.

You are God's Masterpiece,
    "Fearfully and wonderfully made!"
      God's love gives you and me
        A new identity.

<u>We belong to Him!</u>

*****

About the Author

Judy Bowen, the Author of *Riding the Fence Really Hurts*, was "on a fence" of instability, indecision, and waffling for twenty years, unwilling to make a firm choice to obey God, in *all* His ways, and follow His truth exclusively.

During this time, she endured many relationships which were not of God's planning, including two marriages, which only heightened her poor choices and decision to stray from God. But God never gave up on her! Her children, who are living for the Lord, are a testimony to that fact.

God pursued her as a "prodigal" daughter, regardless of toxic and negative circumstances, many of which she created for herself. Throughout all this time, while she continued to believe and trust God's Word, and knew, in her heart, that He loved her unwaveringly, she did not yield to God's call upon her, and refused to align herself with God's abundant plan for her whole life.

After much heartache and confusion, she chose to *finally* get off that hurting fence in 1988, and what a transformation!

About the Author

This new commitment literally framed her life of ministry and testimony. Her expanding outreach to individuals and groups continues today.

As you read more about her journey of riding a fence and eventually yielding completely to God, know that God may be pursuing you, too. He doesn't give up. His love never ceases and He always forgives.

We are reminded of this eternal truth in Romans 8:38-39: KJV (King James Version) [Public Domain]

> [38] For I am persuaded, that neither death, nor life, nor angels, nor principalities, nor powers, nor things present, nor things to come,
> [39] Nor height, nor depth, nor any other creature, shall be able to separate us from the love of God, which is in Christ Jesus our Lord.

Judy's testimony of faith and trust can be an inspiration and motivation for you, our reader, to commit your life wholly to God. He is calling you. That's the focus of this book.

*****

RESOURCES

Resources for beginning a new walk with Christ, or for establishing a richer and more rewarding spiritual life for yourself and others, are readily available to you. Here are some ideas and contacts to consider.

First, find a church that serves your community and preaches/teaches the Word of God, and join a women's or men's Bible study group. Surround yourself with others seeking God's will for their life.

The internet is *full* of resources, daily devotions, online Bible studies, and instructions on how to study the Bible. I recommend this website: www.biblehub.com It contains a wealth of information on the Bible.

Invest in a good Study Bible. I enjoy John McArthur's Study Bible. He's a wonderful theologian who explains the content and context of what you are reading. This writer has spent many careful years studying the scriptures, Hebrew and Greek. All of us *must* stay in the Word of God to increase our faith and trust in Him. The Bible *is* our "daily bread!" Without it, our spiritual lives starve and can eventually die.

Resources

Have on hand the ***Jesus Calling, God Calling, or My Utmost for His Highest*** devotional books. Make it a part of your daily routine to start the day with one of these or more. I order books (used) on www.abebooks.com; these publications are reasonable in price, and in good shape.

Christine Caine is a qualified and amazing teacher, writer, and speaker. I receive her devotions daily in my inbox/email. Please access: www.christinecaine.com.

Faith Gateway Bible Studies and Newsletters: I also receive these daily in my inbox. Please access: www.newsletter@e.faithgateway.com

Hope for the Heart, www.june@hopefortheheart.com is another important resource for me. The author, June, is a wonderful Christian counselor; I've learned much from her. Her book ***Counseling Through Your Bible Handbook***, covers virtually every situation in life, and includes advice and counsel backed by scripture.

Plus, I encourage you to access www.sdrock.com and search **Spiritual Gifts Test**. It only takes about ten minutes and your results in those areas in which you are gifted comes back right away. This helps you in choosing where you want to serve. Also, on this website you can sign up to take the **LIFE Class**. There are four classes, one for each letter: L, I, F, E. Realize your gifts and talents to help you find the best avenue of service in your church or community.

Resources

I've recently added a free app to my phone: **Soulspace** ... This is a five-minute audio meditation designed to slow you down and relax you, reminding you of God's goodness and love for you.

When you come across Bible verses that resonate with you, I encourage you to write them on a 3x5 card and place them on your mirror or fridge to memorize.

There are many more Resources I could list, but this collection is a good start. Fill your heart with Christian music and sermons. Remember: we are what we read, watch, and think about! I'm so excited for you and the path God has planned for you and your spiritual growth!

*****

Products and Services

Products:

Judy Bowen's book, ***Riding the Fence Really Hurts!*** is available through Amazon, on this website: **www.judy-bowen.com** or wherever books are sold.

Services:

Judy is a Bible trainer, a mentor, counselor, teacher, and inspirational speaker. She conducts Bible Studies, ministries in the local Juvenile Hall in San Diego, and is deeply involved in helping to form the Freedom Center in San Diego, California for victims of human trafficking.

She has a rich history of ministry to the staff of one of San Diego's largest and most successful outreach churches, The Rock, pastored by Miles McPherson.

You are warmly invited to contact Judy for in-person presentations to your church, Bible Studies, and more.

Products and Services

*****

Contact Judy Bowen at this website: www.judy-bowen.com

*****

ENDORSEMENT

Brian Carlin, Retired Project Manager and Best-Selling Author

Judy Bowen has been my good friend for around 30 years. I firmly believe that God engineered our friendship because He then used her to guide me back to His arms after I had spent many years wandering lost in the wilderness of agnosticism.

Sometime after becoming friends, a chance remark expressing her faith in God opened the door to my salvation. Now, through telling her own story, Judy can guide the readers of this book, who are likewise lost in the wilderness, to find the loving arms of Jesus.

~ Brian Carlin, Retired Project Manager
Best-Selling Author, 2021

*****

PUBLISHER'S ENDORSEMENT

Glen Aubrey, Creative Team Publishing
www.creativeteampublishing.com
www.glenaubrey.com

Effective leadership, strong and vibrant relationships, investments in lives, integrity, dedication to excellence, and modeling Godly character are a few of the attributes I've witnessed in the life and career of Judy Bowen. A book chronicling Judy's life was suggested to her in 2006, and fifteen later, it has come to pass.

You, one of her readers, will be inspired to not ride a fence of indecision, committed one day and veering from that commitment the next, because waffling really does hurt. Rather, you are invited and encouraged to give yourself to God wholeheartedly, once and for all.

Join Judy on her journey and you may see a mirror on your life in some respects. Living in God's arms and being surrounded by His eternal love and forgiveness await you as you choose to follow God's leading and intervention without reservation.

~ Glen Aubrey, Publisher, Writer, Consultant,
Emmy ® Award Winner, Professional Musician, 2021

THE PUBLISHER

Riding the Fence Really Hurts is published by **Creative Team Publishing, Ft. Worth, Texas**.

www.CreativeTeamPublishing.com

Creative Team Publishing (CTP) is a division of Creative Team Resources Group, Inc. (CTRG). CTP was formed in 2007 to accommodate publication and distribution of business development, leadership training, and poetry books, as well as books of Christian inspiration, insight, human achievement, and positive general interest.

Creative Team Publishing's commitment is to publish high quality literature and engage in excellence throughout the process of publication.

Customer satisfaction is a top priority.
Because CTP practices due diligence in selecting which books it will publish, CTP chooses to work with customers who meet a qualified standard of literary competence and uplifting content.

*****

CPSIA information can be obtained
at www.ICGtesting.com
Printed in the USA
BVHW042240271022
650547BV00005B/41